GOATKEEPING
FOR PROFIT

GOATKEEPING
FOR PROFIT

Jenny Neal

David & Charles
Newton Abbot   London   North Pomfret (Vt)

Photographs by Peter Sumpster
Line drawings by Crispin Neal

British Library Cataloguing in Publication Data

Neal, Jenny
    Goatkeeping for Profit
    1. Livestock: Goats. Production
    I. Title
    636.3'9

    ISBN 0–7153–9065–1

Printed in Great Britain
by Billings & Son, Worcester
for David & Charles Publishers plc
Brunel House Newton Abbot Devon

Published in the United States of America
by David & Charles Inc
North Pomfret Vermont 05053 USA

CONTENTS

5

6

INTRODUCTION

Although people who keep house or show goats have always sold some milk, all too often these sales have been regarded as a bonus towards the cost of feeding animals that are really kept as a hobby. Recently, there has appeared a new breed of goat owner, the commercial goatkeeper. In the past, keeping goats as a business was rather frowned upon by the conventional goat fraternity, although I have never quite understood why. However, commercial goat herds are now respectable and more and more are being established to satisfy the increasing demand for goat products in this country and abroad.

When properly and professionally produced, goats' milk has no significant difference in taste from cows' milk, but has a lighter texture. Its chief advantage lies in the fact that, because of the very small fat globules, it is quickly and easily digested. The fat and protein percentages are similar to cows' milk, but with a higher content of some vitamins and minerals. At present, goats' milk does not need to be pasteurized, so is often the only truly natural raw milk still available to the public. Being very healthy animals, goats normally produce clean milk, and with the increasing interest in unadulterated foods, goats' products are the natural choice. A significant number of people, especially small children for whom milk is a beneficial part of their diet, are allergic to cows' milk. This is probably the most common of the food allergies, and for such people a change to all goats' products can lead to a rapid improvement in health. Goats' milk can be manufactured into a wide range of products like cheese and yogurt, and for the inventive producer the possibilities are endless.

Particularly near large cities there is still a shortage of all these products, which are usually sold through healthfood shops and delicatessens. The prospects are therefore excellent for the budding goat farmer to make a viable business, providing she or he can maintain a reliable supply of top-quality goods.

For goatkeepers who are already fairly experienced, expanding an existing hobby herd would not be too difficult, although they may have to rethink some of their ideas, and take into account new developments in kid-rearing and breeding practices. Those who have little or no previous experience of goats will need to consider both the business and animal husbandry aspects very carefully, and should obtain as much information as possible beforehand. This book offers such potential goatkeepers practical advice, acquired from running a commercial herd of about fifty milkers for some years.

Goats are unique animals, and although they have many things in common with both dairy cows and sheep, they are also quite different from either. Perhaps it goes without saying, but to succeed at a venture like this, it is essential actually to *like* goats; they can be infuriating at times and patience is always needed. Have no fear that, by keeping goats on commercial lines, you will be turning them into factory-farmed animals. Respect for the goats and concern for their welfare at all times is vital, and will result in a happy contented herd, grazing peacefully in the sunshine, or snug in their roomy winter goathouse.

Having read this book and begun your project, I am sure that you will become as involved as I have with these lovable, intelligent animals; but beware—they will take over your life!

CHAPTER ONE

CHOOSING AND BUYING
YOUR GOATS

Although many readers of this book will already be goatkeepers who have some knowledge and a few goats, others will be starting the enterprise from scratch and it is to these that this chapter is mainly aimed.

In order to begin goatkeeping you must first get your goat! People are often inclined to start with just one animal to see how they get on. I would suggest that you try to resist this temptation and obtain at least two. I feel very strongly that goats are so much happier and more well balanced with company of their own kind. Goats are entirely herd animals by nature and their whole behaviour and character is changed and distorted when they are kept alone. You do hear of goats which live alone and seem to be happy, but these are very much the exception. Unless the goat you are buying has been on her own for some time, it would be unfair to take her away from a herd, and, in any case, a single goat would not serve your purpose. Even people owning goats for their own household milk really do need two to keep up a constant supply.

FINDING THE RIGHT ANIMALS

Having decided to begin looking for goats to buy, you will then come up against the most difficult hurdle—how to find suitable stock. It is all too easy to acquire unsatisfactory goats, but much more troublesome to track down what you really need. The breed is not necessarily of primary importance, although for most commercial herds white British Saanen or other Swiss-type goats would be the most likely choice; more about this in Chapter 6.

Firstly, try to resist the temptation to buy goats because you

9

feel sorry for them, such as those seen in markets. Many will not be at all suitable as dairy goats and are being disposed of in this heartless way because they are old, barren or sick. It would have been far kinder for the owner to have sent many of them to the slaughterhouse. It is possible for the experienced goatkeeper to pick up bargains in this manner, but it would be unwise for a beginner to attempt it. The best way to buy goats is by personal recommendation. If you have friends or neighbours with the type of goat you are seeking, ask them if they know of a suitable breeder. This could be the person to whom they take their goats for mating. Owners of stud males often know of goats for sale, sired by their billies and they sometimes have stock to sell themselves.

Breeders of really good pedigree goats quite often have one for sale which does not come up to show standard for one reason or another. Frequently this fault is something trivial from a commercial point of view, such as an incorrect colour or marking. It is always worth contacting the local Goat Society. Every area now has a club affiliated to the British Goat Society who will supply you with the name of the secretary of your nearest club. If you are very new to goats, do not be put off by the attitude of a few members and officials of some clubs, especially when you mention commercial goatkeeping. The negative attitude to profit-making from goats has changed a great deal in the past few years and most of the clubs are now more helpful in this direction. Most of these clubs were developed by, and for, showing people and therefore lean very heavily to that form of goatkeeping. Some societies will have stands at shows where you can obtain leaflets and helpful information, such as breeders' addresses. Do bear in mind however that the show animal is not quite the same as the commercial one, and that the information given out on feeding and housing may not be applicable. Going to a show is an excellent way of seeing the different breeds and getting an idea of what a good, sound goat looks like. The most surprising people sometimes have suitable goats for sale and I once met a judge at a show who was not at all scornful of commercial goatkeeping and subsequently sold me several goats when I was building up my herd.

Having found yourself an honest goat breeder, hopefully on the recommendation of a satisfied buyer, you should place yourself in her hands. (For some reason many goatkeepers are female, so the men will have to forgive me if I often refer to them as 'she'!)

When I have someone wishing to buy a goat or goats from me I attempt to find the right type of goat for them, depending on their requirements. Often if I have nothing suitable at the time, I will know of somebody who has. If possible, try to buy from a herd that is kept under the same sort of conditions as your prospective herd will be. If yours are to be loose-housed, then it would be ideal to purchase them all from one herd if at all possible though unfortunately, goatkeepers rarely have a group to sell all at once. Nowadays there are people who specialise in providing just such groups of milkers or goatlings for new commercial herds, and you may prefer to deal with one of them. It can be very difficult for individual goats to fight their way into the 'pecking order' of an established herd, and this shows up one of the advantages of individual penning.

YOUNGSTOCK

If you are going to have to collect your herd together slowly for a loose-housing system, you may prefer to begin with goatlings or weaned kids. Naturally, you will have to wait longer before establishing your milk production, but there are advantages in starting gently in this manner. When they are still young, goats are not so aggressive towards each other and the hierarchy can be sorted out long before the added stress of kidding and milking comes along.

Young, unweaned kids are also a possibility, and will certainly mix in well together, but you have to be aware of the risk of infectious diseases and parasites being passed from one to another. Try to avoid buying any goat not in the best of health, or a milker who has a very pendulous udder, as these are especially unsuited to machine milking. Goats that are too fat are also to be avoided, especially when not in milk. A fat goat can be very difficult to get in kid, and she may even prove to have always been barren, which could be the reason for her size.

A HEALTHY GOAT

Goats are naturally thin animals and their appearance should be more like that of another good dairy animal, the Jersey cow. They both tend to have a bony back and a large stomach, indicating good food capacity. The difference between a goat who is thin because

11

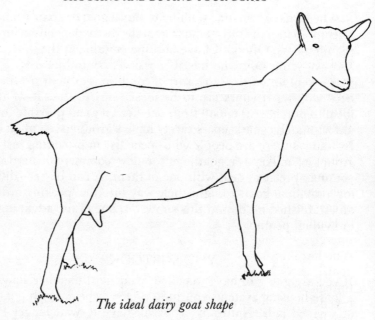

The ideal dairy goat shape

thin because she is milking heavily, and one who is unhealthy, is fairly obvious, even to a beginner. The goat to avoid is the poor, rough-coated creature, with a small, shrunken udder, pale eye membranes, and a 'tucked up' look. Such a goat is often infested with parasites both internal and external, and these may have done so much damage that she would not be a profitable buy.

A healthy goat should have a bright alert look, a sleek shiny coat, with any long hair being of a silky nature and should always be eager for food! It should show a round, well-attached udder with small to medium teats. If you are going to hand milk, you may prefer the teats a little larger, but avoid very divided, badly attached udders.

PEDIGREE OR NON-PEDIGREE

Those setting up a farm goat herd often state that they do not want to bother with pedigree goats and this is perhaps understandable now that it has become so expensive to register kids. I would say that, even if you do not intend to register the kids as you build up your own herd, you would be advised to start with registered stock. These can be goats that are being graded up, in other words, only half, or three-quarters pedigree. The anti-pedigree attitude is understandable among folk who have observed the dreadful deterioration of several dog breeds through bad breeding, and would prefer the healthy 'mongrel'. Thankfully, as goats are productive animals, they have not been bred purely for looks; their show points are also the attributes of a good milker, and milking awards play an important part in the pedigrees of the best goats. Milk production has always been emphasised as being of the utmost importance, and with a registered goat, you will at least have the potential for a good milk yield. They are in no way more delicate than ordinary goats and have usually been well reared to grow into strong adults with a sound body capable of carrying them through many pregnancies and lactations.

Having said all that in praise of the pedigree, there are fine unregistered ones about, and if you have a little knowledge, there is no harm in trying for a bargain. This is less of a risk if a cheap goat is in milk, so that you can at least assess her yield. Many unregistered goats have good pedigree blood in them, but the breeder has not bothered to do the necessary paperwork, so they remain, rather unfairly, the anonymous 'scrub goat'. I would be more wary of buying a goatling, or especially a kid, from stock without papers, as there is such a long time to wait, and much expenditure to be undertaken before their potential is realised.

THE ADVANTAGES OF BUYING KIDS

If, as is likely, you have to buy whatever you can get in the way of milking goats, it is well worth investing, at the same time, in some good-quality youngstock. There are great advantages in beginning with a batch of kids on the bottle or lamb-bar feeder. You can bring them up using your own system, they become accustomed to your management and feeding and are always tame and easily handled. It is a great advantage, if you wish to house all your goats loose, for them to have been brought up together. In addition, if your herd is going to be kept indoors all the time, it is best to begin with animals that were reared inside and are not used to going out to graze. Kids brought up like this never have the desire to go out, never have to contend with weather variations and lead a very healthy productive life later, free from parasitic worms.

In buying kids, there is also the advantage of being able to

13

purchase much better quality youngstock than is possible with older goats. Nobody sells their best goats but they will often offer a kid from such a mother if they have more replacements than they need. You will have a good choice of kids and breeds if you approach the breeders right at the beginning of the kidding season. It is not always easy to judge the quality of a very young kid, but if her sire and dam are a good shape and pedigree, you have the best chance of a good deal. Look particularly at the mother's udder shape. When hand-reared, virtually all kids become tame, placid and calm, but it is not so satisfactory to buy ones which were reared on the dam. Natural rearing sounds a good idea, and has some advantages for the household goatkeeper, but the difference in temperament compared to bottle-fed kids is so striking that it is well worth the extra 'trouble'.

It is also well worth looking out for goatlings, which are goats of one to two years old, who may or may not be in kid. For some unknown reason these can often be bought for less than the cost of rearing them to this age, which can total up to as much as £100. One word of warning: if you are not used to milking goats yet, try to avoid buying mother-reared goatlings as they can be very unco-operative to milk to begin with after kidding. Because of this they are not the best introduction to goatkeeping.

THE LIKELY PRICES FOR GOATS

It is very difficult to be specific about the prices asked for different sorts of goat as prices vary so much in different parts of the country. I can only give you a rough guide, but bear in mind that I am dealing with Westcountry prices which are probably lower than some other regions, and that these were only true at the time of writing. An unregistered or low-grade registered milker may be about £40-£60. Occasionally you can pick up a real bargain for less than this, but few goats under £30 are likely to be worth considering. Many cheaper goats have horns which are nothing but a nuisance. Because of their unpopularity, goats with horns are often very cheap indeed as they are so difficult to sell.

A pedigree milker or in-kid goat is probably going to be between £60 and £80, but you could pay a lot more for prize-winning or milk-recorded stock. A pedigree in-kid goatling would be nearly as much as a milker, having all her productive life before her. Breeders rarely ask a high enough price to cover their rearing costs which makes goats probably the only farm animal to be sold so cheaply. This is a great advantage if you happen to be the buyer!

Kids are even more variable in price, an unregistered one costing very little, but they are best avoided. It costs just as much to rear a low-grade registered kid costing perhaps £15-£20 and this would be a better buy. Full pedigree kids start at about £30 but can be a great deal more if the dam has good milking qualifications.

To sum up, try to obtain the best animals you can, especially if you are only beginning with a small number. If you have to buy several milkers straight away in order to satisfy milk customers, you may have to make do with what you can obtain in a hurry, but do invest in a few better-quality kids or goatlings at the same time. Before you actually go out and buy your goats, please read the next chapter carefully. It is surprising just how many people get the goats first and then wonder where they are going to put them all!

CHAPTER TWO

HOUSING FOR GOATS

THE ADAPTABLE GOAT

Goats are among the most adaptable of animals and can be kept in many different conditions. Think of the nomadic desert goat, apparently living on nothing, the Swiss goat grazing the flower-strewn Alps, the huge herds of yard-fed goats of America, or the pampered show goat of Great Britain. Goats have often been kept on small-holdings as part of a mixed enterprise, but in recent years a few farmers have realised the potential of the dairy goat and thus the new breed of British goat farmer has emerged. So far the goat is mercifully free from restrictions, milk quotas and heavy-handed officialdom.

There has been an attitude, among some goatkeepers, that their particular style of management is the right one and that everyone else is keeping their goats badly. Logically, this cannot be true, but unfortunately goats are sometimes kept in appalling conditions, half starved and neglected. Nobody would defend that type of owner, and thankfully, the good ones are far more prevalent than the bad. As long as the basic needs of food, shelter and good management are supplied, there is no 'right' and 'wrong' way to accommodate goats.

Newcomers to goatkeeping may be confused by conflicting advice, particularly if they read other books. Some authors suggest that goats must have daily exercise, whatever the weather; others that they must never go out in the rain. Few suggest what you do when it rains all day, every day, for several days! I suspect that they do not live in the areas of the country where this is likely, or even inevitable. There is a school of thought that says the goat house should be warm, and another that states that no heating should be required. The new owner may be convinced that she is doing all the wrong things and the goats will suffer. When I went to buy my first goats I was afraid that the old stone barn in which I intended to house them was not good enough. However, when I saw the decrepit corrugated pig-sties that they came from, I was much happier.

As I suggested in the previous chapter, kids are more adaptable to a new home and different system, so if buying adults, attempt to obtain them from homes with similar management. This is especially applicable if you are going to have to tether your milkers, although this is the least satisfactory way of providing grazing and is very time consuming for the commercial herd. After you have kept goats for a while you may wish to change your ideas, for instance, by switching from grazing to stall-feeding, or free-range instead of tethering. Goats that are used to free-range grazing will take to stall-feeding better if it is introduced during the winter when most goats spend much time indoors anyway.

STALL-FEEDING

Stall-feeding, also called zero-grazing, means keeping goats indoors all the time and bringing all their food to them. It does *not* imply that the goat is tied immobile in a stall all day, and many will also have access to a concrete yard outside. The term comes from the days when horses were nearly all kept tied in stalls and some of the early goat breeders adopted a 'mini' version of the horse stall. It was found to be a very successful system, because in the days before good worm medicines, small paddocks became heavily infested and 'goatsick'. The goats were seen to thrive much better indoors, although I suspect, at that time, few people realized the reason. Just as stalls have largely been replaced by loose-boxes for horses, stall-fed goats are now kept in individual pens, or all running together in spacious accommodation. A small, concrete outdoor exercise yard is a very useful, although not an essential asset to the plan. To have peace of mind when you are out, this yard must be securely fenced to a height of 4ft (1.2m).

This is a very efficient form of goatkeeping, particularly suited to those who are only part-time smallholders and are out at work for long periods. Very large farm herds also employ it as a way of encouraging a steady yield of milk all the year round and keeping the goats free from worms. The goats are protected at all times from the elements, none of their food is wasted by trampling, and with the use of well-designed racks for green food and hay, goats can

17

be kept almost anywhere even if the owner has little or no land.

HOUSING FOR THE SMALL HERD

If land is available (a worthwhile amount would be 2–5 acres for a small herd of up to ten milkers) goats can obtain much of their summer food for themselves. If they are going to be out a great deal their pens, and the goathouse therefore, need not be as large and sophisticated as for the zero-grazed herd. A good roof over their heads will be needed, plenty of fresh air, and accommodation large enough to be comfortable when they are inside in winter. Individual pens for single goats should be about 5 x 5ft (1.5 x 1.5m). If you have two friendly goats together in a pen, it only needs to be a little larger. When it comes to loose-housing it is difficult to be precise, as it all depends on the numbers involved. Suffice it to say, there should be little squabbling, the goats should have room to lie down a little apart from each other if they wish, and must all be able to line up at the long hay rack with enough room to eat in peace. Observation and common sense are the best way to determine the exact number of goats a given area can accommodate.

Let us first consider the type of housing suited to the small herd, consisting of up to perhaps ten milkers, who are probably going to be milked by hand. This would be the typical smallholding enterprise and you may have to utilise existing buildings or build from scratch as inexpensively as possible. Later I will deal with the farm-sized herd as its needs are slightly different (see page 24).

Many materials can be used for goathouse construction, but inevitably, most people will have no choice but to adapt an existing building. Most buildings can be used for goats—sheds, stables, pig-sties, even large dog kennels and hound yards. Goats have even been kept in caravans, but these are not ideal, not least owing to the unsightly appearance of the structures. The wooden flooring is quite unsuitable and the goats will certainly attempt to eat the fibreglass lining material, with disastrous results. Unless you are on very quick-draining land, it is essential to have a concrete floor, or something equally as hard such as the cobbles or bricks found in old stables. If concrete is not possible, materials such as clinker, gravel or chalk can be rammed down to form a hard surface. The milking area must be completely washable if you are going to be selling milk. As goats are normally kept on deep litter, a drain as such will not work, but a slight slope will help to keep the bed dry.

If you are able to build a goathouse especially for the purpose, try to plan ahead and make it bigger than you feel you need, or of such a design that you can add on later. Building a goathouse is like buying a deep freeze—you always wish you had a bigger one!

LOOSE-HOUSING OR INDIVIDUAL PENS

Deciding whether the occupants are to be in pens or loose-housed is the first step, or you may compromise and have them in small batches together. It may be that your existing buildings dictate to you. If you have a run of stables in a row, you would probably keep two or three goats to a stable. Should you be converting a large building such as a Nissen hut, then it would be easier to divide it into two large pens with a central passage. In the case of loose-housing, consider how you are going to cater for individual concentrate feeding. Perhaps you will only feed these at milking time. Otherwise you need an arrangement usually known as a 'heck' in which the goats are held by the neck in a row while they eat.

BUILDING MATERIALS

When building, it is economical to take advantage of whatever materials are available locally. The builder may have some preference and some districts have by-laws controlling the use of materials. Naturally you will want to have a tidy-looking building which blends in with the environment, and this would normally be a planning requirement if you live in a National Park. Existing farms and smallholdings can usually put up farm buildings without planning permission in most places, but it is always worth checking first.

The most likely materials are concrete block or wood. The latter is very suitable for small constructions, being warm, pleasing to the eye and fairly cheap if bought second hand. If using old doors and windows, do ensure that all the old paint is burnt off. Goats always chew wood and the lead contained in old paint is deadly. Treating all bare wood with creosote or other wood preservative before you put the goats in the building will discourage this chewing. Creosote appears to be safe for goats as long as it is dry before they come in contact with it. One material that can often be obtained cheaply are the outer planks from a sawn tree. These are known as outshells, or scalings, but may have other names in different districts. When nailed overlapping, they make an attractive wall to a goathouse and will last for many years if frequently treated. A tanalised timber building will last much longer and many firms now make buildings from this material ready to be erected on your concrete base.

The roof can be constructed from any modern roofsheet material, second-hand corrugated iron being the cheapest. Naturally, look for undamaged sheets and, when you put the roof on, make sure that the existing nail-holes are on the upper convex surface, not the lower convex one, in order to avoid leaks. If possible allow at least one transparent roof sheet in a small goathouse, or more in a larger one, to provide light, but do not have too many in a small building, or you will be building a greenhouse instead!

Windows, Doors and Ventilation
A simple shed or loose box should have a stable-type door to provide light and air and allow the goats to see out. If they tend to jump, a bar can be fixed across the upper half, as the top door will normally be kept open, at least in the day time. In larger buildings windows are needed which can be left open for most of the time. The glass will have to be protected with a wire mesh screen inside the window frame which remains in place when the window is open.

It is rarely necessary to shut all doors and windows as goats need plenty of fresh air. Naturally, the door and, if possible, windows should face away from the prevailing winds, which will vary according to local conditions in your part of the country. I read once that the door of a goathouse should face south-west, presumably for the sun. If this advice was followed in south-west England, the door would have to be shut very frequently to prevent the rain from beating in on the occupants! The answer is to observe your own conditions and the aspect of neighbouring farm buildings before deciding on the best position.

Many goats are kept in too hot and stuffy conditions and these are not good for them. Ventilate the accommodation as much as possible in all but the most severe weather. Providing that they are not in a direct draught, or getting wet, goats, like all ruminants, are

20

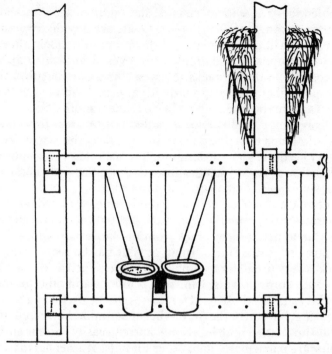

The front view of a goat pen

very resistant to low temperatures and should never be kept in a fug.

PEN CONSTRUCTION AND EQUIPMENT

For pen divisions within the house, either timber, concrete block or welded wire mesh can be used. If using slatted wood the bars must either be very close together, so that the goats cannot push their heads through at all, or very wide apart so that there is no risk of them getting stuck. The bars should be horizontal rather than vertical as goats can push right through upright bars easily and love doing so, unfortunately sometimes with fatal results. Kids especially should not be kept in pens with vertical bars as their heads are only a little wider than their bodies, enabling them to escape without difficulty. Goats should be able to see each other easily but must not be able to lean right over to steal the next goat's hay, or bully her so that she is afraid to eat.

In each pen, or between two, should be a hay rack made from

21

welded mesh or wooden slats. If slatted, then the slats should be no more than 4in (10cm) apart. Goats are dreadfully wasteful of hay, and will pull a great deal down onto the floor, after which they look upon it disdainfully, however clean it may appear. It is possible to design racks to catch this waste, but they take up a great deal of room in an individual pen. A simple welded mesh hay rack can be fitted with a lid to make it more difficult for large wedges of hay or silage to be pulled out. A great time-saver is a rack designed to be filled from the outside of the pen, essential for larger herds. If you are designing from scratch you will be able to take all such considerations into account, but with a ready-made building you may have to compromise.

For loose-housing, very long racks running the whole length of a pen are usually provided, and any person who can weld will easily be able to make such a rack from the large hay panels available at farmers' goods stores. In an outside yard a really large robust rack is very useful for feeding bulky things such as whole kale and Brussels sprout plants, fruit-tree prunings and other branches.

Hay nets like those used for horses can be useful as a temporary measure, but can be dangerous because, unlike horses, goats like to stand up on their hind legs to eat, and can easily become entangled. They are particularly dangerous for kids. If a net *has* to be used it may be safer to hang it on the outside of the pen so that the goat eats through the bars.

The other equipment you need for individual pens includes a bucket or bowl for concentrates and another for water. It is a great help if all the feeding and watering can be done without opening the gate and entering each pen. This can easily be arranged by having the goat put her head out of a hole or slats in the gate and eating from a bucket held in place by a bucket ring. Not only does this save time, but you can see whether the goat is eating up well, or leaving some of her food. A double ring can be used to hold both feed and water, both remaining cleaner than when in the pen with her and they cannot be readily knocked over. Goats have an uncanny knack of filling their water buckets with droppings, and although they can still do it with the bucket on the outside of the gate, it takes much more skill on their part! Male goats like to top up their 'water' while standing with their front feet up on the gate! It is small wonder that male goats have a reputation for being poor drinkers.

Goats like to climb up on something to sleep, and if there is room would appreciate a small wooden bench for this purpose. It is easier to arrange for this in communal housing when a row of pallets would suffice.

FACILITIES FOR YOUNGSTOCK AND MILKING

Separate accommodation for baby kids and young growing goats is required, as it is usual for commercial goatkeepers to keep the kids well away from the rest of the herd. The reasons will be explained in Chapter 8 and at the same time I will suggest some suitable arrangements for housing them. Once the kids are about six to nine months old they can, if necessary, move into pens alongside the milkers, ready to mix with the herd. If they are going to have to fight their way into entirely communal housing with older goats, I would wait until they are a little older and introduce them all at once so that the bullying of an individual goatling will be minimized.

One facility that is absolutely necessary is a separate area for milking, and a proper dairy for washing up, handling and packing the milk. These areas will be described more fully in Chapter 11.

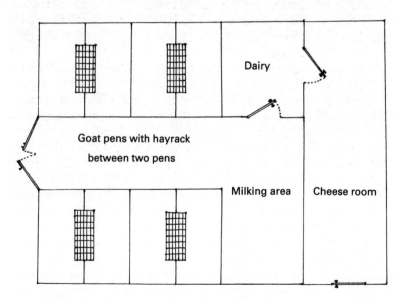

Design for a small goathouse; further pens can be easily added on

23

For the moment it is enough to say that it aids management a great deal if the milking 'parlour' (even if it is only a sectioned-off part of the goathouse) is adjoining the main building. If necessary the dairy can be a room in your house.

ADAPTING FARM BUILDINGS

For the farmer who already has potentially suitable unused buildings, I would suggest that he visits as many goat farms as possible to pick up ideas. There will be some who are able to spend a great deal of capital at the outset and can have everything perfect at once, housing, yards, fencing, milking parlour etc. There will be many more who have had to make do with what was there already, and have done a good job in adapting places like deep-litter poultry houses, cow cubicle houses, and calf houses. Cow milking parlours are built entirely to the wrong scale and would need drastic alteration.

Most larger herds use the loose-housed system with anything from ten to fifty goats to an area. If you intend to feed silage rather than hay, a central passage in the building with a barrier through which the goats can put their heads may be better than overhead racks. A long trough can be used for silage, chopped roots or even concentrates if communally fed. For such a herd, an automatic water system is a must. Providing that they are kept clean, goats will drink fresh cold water readily from bowl drinkers on the wall. Some farmers have arrangements to tap the heat from milk-cooling systems to provide warm water for goats to drink and this certainly improves their intake.

To sum up, a goathouse should be wind- and watertight, but with adequate ventilation. It should have a dry floor with ample bedding, there should be no overcrowding and access to food should be made easy. Providing all these requirements are met, almost any sort of building can be adapted by the handy person. If you are not handy, then ready-made buildings are available.

CHAPTER THREE

CONTROL AND FENCING

Having decided on the method of housing your goats, and hopefully prepared everything before their arrival, the question of control can no longer be ignored, assuming that you are going to put them out to graze.

THE WANDERING GOAT

I am sorry to say that the bad reputation that the goat has of breaking out and eating everything in sight is, to some extent, true. Because of this habit, people sometimes have the erroneous idea that as 'goats eat everything', they can survive on next to nothing. This could not be further from the truth for the goat has an enormous appetite and need for proper bulk food. This can most easily be supplied during summer by good grazing. Given the opportunity, goats would wander at will all over the countryside, taking a snatch here and a mouthful there all day until dark or milking time. Although this is possible in regions more traditionally inhabited by goats, this cannot be allowed in a developed country such as this. All land is owned by somebody and fields are carefully cultivated to provide feed for stock. Although goats will utilise almost any kind of vegetation from moorland heather, coppice woodland or roadside verges and hedges, they generally milk best on properly managed mixed grass pasture. This is where the question of fencing comes in; the grass must be yours and not a neighbouring farmer's. He will not be pleased to find several greedy goats munching their way through his crop of silage grass! He may perhaps turn a blind eye if they are removing the brambles from the hedge, or nipping the tops off seeding nettles and thistles, but the principle is still the same. Your goats have no right on any land other than your own without previous permission. An owner may of course give

25

that permission when he sees their taste for what he considers pestilential weeds.

All this means that, unless you live in the midst of common land over which you have grazing rights, you must control your goats. The law is quite clear on this point that it is your duty to fence your own stock in securely, not that of others to keep them out.

TETHERING

The traditional way of controlling goats is by tethering. Although this has a few advantages, such as being able to utilise odd corners and verges, it has far more disadvantages and is generally unsatisfactory, especially for the goat. Obviously it is better for any animal to be free to move about at will than to be permanently attached to a fixed point. The main reason that 'respectable' goatkeepers dislike tethering is that it can so easily be abused by lazy people and is rarely done well. You will all have seen the miserable sight of a goat tied and probably entangled by the roadside, alone and out in all weathers until her owner returns to fetch her after work and obtain his 'free' milk. If you do go out to work, then a system of stall-feeding with tethering only at weekends and on summer evenings is practical. Goats staked out in unsuitable spots are completely at the mercy of hot sun, driving rain, and the torments of roaming dogs and vandals.

Kids should never be tethered and the British Goat Society states as much in their code of practice. Free kids are extremely agile and playful, constantly twisting, leaping and jumping on and off objects, rarely seeming to hurt themselves. As soon as they are put on a tether all this changes and they are constantly at risk of becoming caught and entangled with fatal results. If kids are being reared on their mothers they stay close to her at first, but sooner or later will venture further afield and get into mischief. As soon as the kids begin popping into the garden to sample the flowers, the exasperated owner is liable to sentence them to a tether. In all too many cases it is a sentence of death. Tragedy often occurs when the kid runs and jumps with a twist, coming to a sudden terrible jerk at the end of the chain. Commercial kids on the other hand are usually reared artificially, when they can be either housed entirely, or have a yard or securely fenced paddock of their own.

Tethering can be used carefully and wisely in certain circumstances, such as for controlling several stud males when they have to be kept apart from the females. Also, it quite often happens that when you get your first few goats, your fencing may not yet be up to scratch, and tethering is a reasonable way to begin. In these circumstances it is best that you have adult goats who are accustomed to being tied.

If you should have to tether, please try not to economise by doing without the proper equipment. Nylon rope, while strong and cheap, makes an unsatisfactory tether because it tangles so easily around the goat's legs and can cause rope burns and sores where it cuts in. Being light, it also snags round small shrubs and weeds leaving the goat fixed in one spot until someone comes to disentangle her. Use a purpose-made chain tether purchased from one of the goat equipment firms. It will be about 15ft (4.5m) long with at least two swivels and a strong spring clip at the end. A heavy chain like this will slide down her legs more easily if it should become wound up, enabling her to step out of it.

Another essential piece of equipment is a proper leather collar, wide enough not to cut into her neck and strongly stitched. Goats are often seen wearing plaited nylon bale-twine collars, which are most unsuitable for tethering as they can so easily twist on the neck like a tourniquet. Goats have 'pressure points' on either side of the neck, which, if compressed hard, will cause the animal to fall to the ground twitching. This sometimes happens while a goat is being led, especially if she is pulling and resisting, wanting to go somewhere different. The pressure can be released immediately in this case, and the goat will completely recover in a few seconds. If the pressure is kept up though, as with an unsuitable collar, or if the goat should fall down the far side of a bank while tethered, the result can be fatal.

It is not always easy to find a good stake for hammering into the ground as it needs to be strong. It should be in the form of a metal rod about 20in (0.5m) long and with a knob on one end. Corkscrew-type dog tethers are rarely strong enough. For our tethered stud males, who are very strong, we use heavy old tyres from a tractor or lorry. The chain will not entangle and they can be moved by turning on end and rolling to a new position. There is nothing on a tyre to injure a goat and the males love to stand up on their tyres to survey the herd more easily.

One of the biggest problems of keeping goats outside in Britain, whether tethered or free, is the unpredictability of the weather.

Goats are not delicate, but they dislike heavy rain intensely, as they have no waterproofing in their coats. The odd summer shower does not harm them, but they should not be left out in winter, unless the weather is unusually mild, or you live in a very sheltered spot like a wooded valley. Some enterprising people have made coats for their goats from light waterproof canvas like the New Zealand rugs worn by outdoor horses in winter. These would be most useful for days when you are not sure what the weather is going to be like.

THE IMPORTANCE OF EFFICIENT FENCING

If you decide that either stall-feeding or tethering is not for you because you prefer to see your goats running free, you will then have to consider fencing. Any existing fencing around your land is unlikely to be goatproof, however effective it is for cattle, horses or even sheep. Goats jump if they have a clear view of the other side, otherwise they climb, scramble or push their way through anything. They do not escape from fields because they are short of grass, but because they *can*, so do not be fooled into thinking they will not go wandering if there is ample vegetation. It seems to be the challenge and adventure that lures them to the other side and even when the next-door field is ploughed earth, they will still break through if they can. It is a mistake to think that any kind of hedge will contain them for long, but a very thick overgrown one may be successful for a while, providing plenty of browsing in the meantime. Some goats are more adventurous than others, and you are fortunate indeed if all your goats are the stay-put type!

The biggest problem with any type of fencing is the cost, and there is no cheap way of doing it unless you are only making a small secure yard where second-hand timber can be used. The smaller the area the goats have access to, the more secure it will need to be as the fence will be under more constant pressure from the goats than one surrounding a larger acreage. You must have at least one field completely goat-proof so that you can go out without worry. Nothing is more annoying than having to keep goats in during a fine day because you cannot rely on the fencing. When I had my first goats, I tried everything, tethering, relying on the hedge, electric fencing, stock netting mesh with a solid pole along the top, and finally the most successful of all, stock netting with an electric wire above.

28

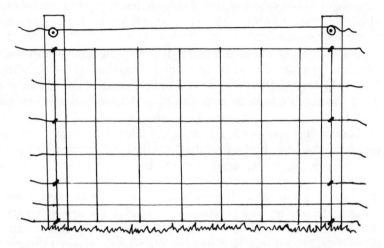

Stock fencing with electric wire on insulators above the fence

Permanent fencing

For a small paddock, well-erected chain-link is suitable, or 'motorway' fencing, which is a combination of post and rail and stock netting. Both of these are expensive but will cope well with goats standing on them. A cheap imitation of motorway fencing can be made with rough forestry poles rather than tanalised sawn timber.

The least expensive wire netting appears to be the heavy, square-holed wire, usually known as stock netting. This can be obtained with a height of 1m or there is a slightly taller one, which would really be better for goats if the extra cost can be borne. But even if this is put up well by a fencing contractor, or someone else with the proper straining tools, the goats will pull it down sooner or later by standing up with their front feet on it. Eventually it will sag enough for the goats to scramble over. Sheep netting, which looks like large mesh chicken wire, is even worse, as the wires are not strong enough to resist goats standing on them for even a few months. Holes will appear, through which goats will push their heads and wherever a goat's head will go, sooner or later the body will surely follow! For either type of wire fence, something is needed to prevent sagging. A wooden pole or rail can be used, but just as effective, more long-lasting and probably cheaper in the long run, is a single strand of electric fencing. This should run about 6in above the top of the wire, on nail-on insulators attached to the wooden posts.

A common mistake with fencing is to use short posts and have them too far apart. This is a false economy, as is using non-tanalised posts. However well you think you have creosoted them, they are bound to rot and have to be replaced sometime in the future, especially if your land lies wet. Posts should be between 6 and 8ft (1.8 and 2.4m) apart and tall enough to allow 1ft (30 cm) to stand up above the wire. If you find that you have a show-jumping goat you can add more insulators and another strand of wire.

Stock fencing, especially if erected by a contractor, will usually have barbed wire along the top and you may be wondering why all this electric fencing is necessary. This is because goats and barbed wire *do not mix*. Goats have absolutely no respect for anything prickly and totally disregard the fencing power of barbed wire. Sooner or later goats will always attempt to jump or climb over this type of fence, with a disastrous effect on the udder. It is not possible to state that barbed wire must never be used when there are goats about, because this is not practical on a mixed holding where cattle are kept. You can compromise, as we do, by disconnecting and preferably winding up the electric wire when cattle are using a field, and replacing the electric fencing when the goats are there, to prevent them thinking about jumping.

If you have a registered smallholding or farm, you may be able to get a grant for permanent fencing. The amount of this grant varies considerably depending partly on where you live, so telephone your local Ministry of Agriculture office for details.

Electric Fencing
Much less expensive than this permanent fence is electric fencing alone, particularly useful for larger farms where there are several fields available to the goat herd at different times of the year. Nowadays there are many different systems and it may be worth finding a specialist firm to advise you on the best type for your situation. I have not found farmers' goods stores very good at advising on these matters although they sell all the materials. Properly maintained and working effectively electric fencing is excellent, but it is no use thinking that you can confine

goats behind a single strand like a herd of cows. If only it were that simple!

When I first experimented with my goats many years ago, I made every mistake under the sun. I found that the two strands, as advised in a book, were insufficient unless directly in front of another fence. The fencer unit was not really powerful enough and the goats would take a chance on sliding underneath. Using it around the field boundary was quite good but it was a constant battle to prevent wet vegetation from shorting it. Now there are much better units that give a really good shock even with some growth touching the bottom wire. Mains models and those run from car batteries seem to work better in this respect than those using dry batteries. The latter are also much more expensive to run. It may seem cruel to talk of a 'good shock', but it is really being cruel to be kind, for if they get a powerful shock they may never go near it again. Once they have learnt to respect the fence, goats can have the benefit of a free-range life.

Other goatkeepers use the electrified sheep netting to good effect, being light and easy to move and put up. We have never been able to get it to work properly as our grass is usually too long and lush. You really need to trim underneath with a strimmer to avoid losing electrical power to the wet grass. It is probably the only electric fencing suitable for kids.

A new system available now, which we make use of and find very good, is a set of plastic posts with little hooks at intervals all the way up. This means that you can have as many strands as you like and in various positions. We use two or three strands, and find it particularly useful to reinforce the hedge in fields which are only periodically used by goats. Another innovation is a permanent electric fence, using a special type of wooden post and high tensile wire. I have not seen it in use on a farm, but from its appearance when shown on trade stands at agricultural shows, I would think it would be very difficult, if not impossible, for a goat to get through. Naturally it would not be cheap, but because it is classed as permanent fencing, it would be grant-aided.

Fencing Kids

Kids are, as I have mentioned, the most difficult age group to fence, and if you wish to have them out with the herd, you will probably have to use the proper stock netting fence. Even this is sometimes a problem, because if you rear horned kids, perhaps for meat, or have other horned goats such as Angoras, they can get their heads stuck in the square mesh. Kids seem to delight in forcing their heads through seemingly impossible holes and, with horns, are quite unable to get them back. It is even difficult for the owner, having discovered them, to manipulate the head back the way it came. Yet another reason why most commercial herds house their kids!

In the old days people used to take goats out into the countryside and herd them about to feed. This entailed someone being with them all day, and few folk can spare so much time these days. If you have a very small number of goats and permission to graze them, you could take them out in this way, perhaps into an overgrown wood that is due for felling. It would be rare, though, for the commercial goatkeeper to be able to spare the time.

FIELD SHELTERS

I have already referred to the undesirability of leaving tethered goats out in the rain, but perhaps you are wondering about free-range goats? We find that ours do not mind light summer drizzle or showers, but if it comes on to rain heavily they will want to come in after a while. If you are able to provide some kind of field shelter for them to take cover in while the shower lasts, you will be able to make use of your grazing for longer in the year. The shelter need not be elaborate, but must be large enough for them all to get in comfortably. This is a problem with really large herds, as the cost of another substantial building would be great. Another alternative is for the goats to be free to come back to their own house at will, perhaps along a fenced passageway from the paddock. Again, this would be impractical for the farm with many fields and when a large number of goats is involved, the passage would become very muddy. Like so many aspects of goatkeeping, it is all a matter of trial and error and finding out what is best for your farm and your goats.

CHAPTER FOUR

FEEDING GOATS

There is a commonly held but erroneous belief that goats will eat anything. Ask almost anyone about goats and they will repeat this fallacy. In addition they will tell you that they make 'good lawnmowers'; 'get a goat and you will be able to say goodbye to that tedious summer task of grass cutting'. At the same time you will be informed that they rid your garden of weeds too! It is interesting to note that it is invariably people who have had very little or nothing at all to do with goats, who profess to be so knowledgeable in these matters. Those with a wide experience of the proper care of goats know that all this is far from the truth, and that while goats will sample almost any green growing plant, they must have a correct nutritious diet of bulk food, and plenty of it. Grass as short as the average lawn, even when overgrown, is of little use to them, and will only be eaten roughly and unevenly at best. Far from selectively devouring all your weeds, goats will certainly head for the roses first. After that, like as not, they will start on the poisonous laburnum and become ill. Even a garden that needs 'eating down' has to be fenced (see Chapter 3), and how are the goats to be fed when everything is grazed down?

The aim of the goatkeeper is to provide as much natural bulk feed as possible, usually in the form of grass and hay, with added concentrate food for milk production. Weeds and titbits from the garden can be looked upon only as extras. It is quite amazing just how much bulk food a goat consumes in a day. The goat is a ruminant, which means that she has four stomachs, one of which, the rumen, is a large vat in which she can pack away large quantities of grass as she eats rapidly. This will later be brought up to be re-chewed. The goat's rumen is larger in proportion to her size than that of any other domestic ruminant, and as a result she can have a very bloated appearance after a day's grazing. Providing that she is chewing the cud happily, everything is working, and she will gradually deflate during the night. This large stomach enables goats to live on apparently very poor pasture in desert areas, as they are able to pack in such a quantity of low-quality fibrous food in order to get the necessary nutrients. In addition to this, there is a wide range of plant foods acceptable to them, and they are always willing to experiment.

HAY FEEDING

In Britain the basic food for stall-fed goats, and for all goats in winter, has been hay. Now, increasingly, when a larger herd is kept, silage, often of the big-bale type, is used. I will deal with hay feeding first as it is still by far the most usual food, and one whose importance can hardly be overstated.

A goat who lives indoors all the time will need at least 5lb (2 kg) of hay a day, assuming she has little or no green food, and depending on other feeds used. If you are able to feed hay ad lib, you will find that some goats will eat much more than 5lb (2 kg). In practice, this means a bale of hay per goat, per week, enabling you to plan ahead and work out how much hay you will need for the year. Naturally, bales vary in size, but roughly this works out to about one ton of hay for each goat for a year. This sounds an awful lot, but it is better to budget for this amount, as you can never have too much. It is unfortunate to run out late in the winter when you may not be able to get the right quantity and the price is sure to be high.

For goats on good grazing for about eight months of the year, half this amount of hay may be sufficient. In summer and spring, and even into the autumn, when they have ample grazing, goats often eat only very little hay at night. If you are able to allow your herd out at night in good weather as well, you could save even more, but it is important that the grass be plentiful in this case.

If you stall-feed, but have a little land to use for growing goat crops, you can substitute some green food for hay. Do not make the mistake of thinking that a few kale leaves or a handful of carrots will constitute an adequate replacement though. Green food is largely water and this must be taken into account when considering its feed value.

Once you have worked out your hay requirements, you will need to obtain the hay. If you have sufficient land to put one or two fields aside, you could make your own. If you have no machinery it is usually possible to find an agricultural contractor who is prepared to undertake small jobs, and who may also help you to bring it in. Quite a number of small goatkeepers have obliging neighbours who will make their hay for them, but this does not always work out well. Neighbours can only be called upon to attend to your hay when they have cleared their own, and there is sometimes embarrassment about payment for the job. On the whole it is advisable to have a proper agreement with someone who does contracting work regularly and who will have a set price per hour or per acre.

Buying Hay

Many goatkeepers will have to buy hay, either because they have insufficient land, or have difficulty in making the really high-quality hay that goats require. If possible, should you have spare grass, it is worth making a little hay, if only because of the beneficial effect of cutting to the land. On the whole, when buying hay, it can be best to go to a merchant, especially if you are inexperienced. As with all matters, it is best to go to one recommended to you. A local dealer will have a reputation to keep, and you may be able to find one who is used to supplying hay for horses or calves, in other words, one who is used to dealing with fairly small customers and whose hay is of good quality.

The importance of having palatable hay for goats cannot be over-stressed. However much 'rubbish' they may eat in the way of weeds, branches, rushes and bark, it does not follow that they eat bad hay. The slightest mould or mustiness will cause them to reject it, so do not deal with a merchant who tries to palm you off with something poor because 'it is only for goats'. If possible try to obtain a sample bale first to try it out on the goats. If you can discover an honest reliable merchant, half your worries will be over, as he will always be in a position to seek out supplies for you.

However, if you decide to buy hay directly off the field in summer it will be much cheaper, but beware, it is not always the bargain it seems. It will lose weight during storage and the snag is that you cannot always be sure that it was properly dry when baled. New hay has to be stored very carefully so that it can continue to dry out, and a Dutch barn style of building with open sides is really needed. New hay stacked in small loads of less than a couple of tons tends to deteriorate more quickly. This is made much worse by being stored in a closed building when it becomes sweaty and damp and mould soon develops. It is very disappointing to find that your hay is nearly all useless, when you thought you had plenty for the winter. It is no use complaining to the farmer from whom you bought it when this happens, but when dealing with a merchant, you are paying for his skill and judgement in obtaining hay for you that will store well. If hay is delivered already mouldy you can refuse to accept it, but if it becomes mouldy after you have had it for some time, you are usually stuck with it. This mould is dangerous to your health and that of your goats and should not be inhaled.

Types of Hay
A great deal of nonsense is written about hay for goats. In my experience it is not the type of grass that the hay was made from that matters, but the flavour and palatability of the finished product. In other words, it must have been well made, without rain, and kept well, so that it has a sweet clean scent without a trace of mustiness. In older books on goats, and occasionally newer ones, it is stressed that goats must have clover hay. This is not grass with clover in it, but a crop of clover or lucerne grown specially, and is coarse and of a rather brownish colour. This hay is virtually unobtainable now, at least in the western and northern part of the country. It used to be grown in East Anglia, and may possibly still be available there. It always was expensive as it has a high feed value, but now the cost of transporting it to other parts of Britain would make it totally uneconomical to use. If you cannot obtain it, do not worry; thousands of goats manage quite well without it, and if you wish to use a really high-value product, try barn dried hay. This is not easy to obtain either, but is worth hunting out. This hay is cut early in the summer, partially made in the field as normal, but then dried out with hot air in a building. Usually it is excellent, with a lovely smell, and because it was made when the grass was at a perfect stage of growth, can be very nutritious. It is worth keeping some for freshly kidded goats.

Another desirable product is known as 'seeds' hay, which is made from a specially grown ley of grass or grass and clover. This is often early maturing rye-grass, which can be cut early. Like all hay, if it is well made, the value should be good. I have read that goats do not like rye-grass hay, yet one of the best loads we ever bought was pure rye-grass seeds hay, which the goats loved. It had a coarse texture, which made it difficult for the goats to pull out of the racks, thereby reducing waste.

Most hay for sale is meadow hay, which can mean almost anything. It can be made from permanent or semi-permanent ley consisting of one or two grasses and perhaps clover, or it can be from old 'unimproved' pasture. The latter could be very rough grassland, containing a great number of thistles, docks and other weeds. Providing that it is dry and sweet, this will be acceptable to goats. They will enjoy the weeds, but bear in mind that the feed value is unlikely to be very high, and it may have been cut late. Goats, being rather contrary creatures who do not always read the nutrition books, often do better when allowed ad-lib hay of this type, just because they like it. Quality *is* important, especially if you do not feed a lot of concentrates, but I think that goats' personal quirks should be taken into account. If you can obtain at least some of your hay from this type of old, unsprayed traditional meadow, the goats will benefit from the diversity of wild plants. Digestive problems, mineral problems and other complaints of high yielding animals can often be avoided by the presence of natural herbs in the pasture or hay.

BIG-BALE SILAGE

There is really only one universal alternative to hay and one which is especially suited to the larger smallholding or small farm, where you are able to make your own fodder. This is big-bale silage. It is possible to use ordinary clamp silage for goats, such as is made for dairy cows, but it has to be very well made and rather drier than usual. Clamp silage is also difficult to make in small quantities, but the invention of big-bale silage in recent years has made all the difference. We have changed over to it completely for all our goat feeding and I have nothing but praise for the system, and the goats love it. As with haymaking, if you use your own grass, but have a contractor to do all the mechanical work for you, it is still considerably cheaper than buying in hay, even after taking the contractor's costs into account. It is also much easier than making hay in a high rainfall area, or during a bad summer.

Big-bale silage is made by cutting the grass at the normal hay stage, turning once and drawing into rows, after which the baler makes it into very large round bales. The whole process takes only about two or three days and the weather does not have to be really hot and sunny as for haymaking. Because of the size (the bales weigh about 8 cwt), they are moved by means of a tractor with a spike on the front loader, and brought to the farm buildings to be enclosed in black plastic bags. Once the bags are on, the bales are stacked and fastened to make them airtight, and left for at least six weeks before use. The stack must be well weighted down with a nylon net thrown over, to prevent wind damage to the plastic. The product that comes out, providing that no damage has occurred to the seal, is quite dry, between 45 and 60 per cent dry matter, and very sweet smelling. When feeding you will have to give slightly more than hay to account for the higher percentage of water. If you have a tractor you can move a bale at a time to the goathouse, otherwise it is quite feasible to cut the bag off and take the bale apart in situ and load the silage into a wheelbarrow. It is also possible to roll the bales a short way, preferably downhill! Providing that it is a fairly dry silage, the opened bales will remain good for up to two weeks. Each bale is roughly the equivalent of twelve bales of hay, so if you are feeding that amount in less than two weeks, it would be worth considering this silage instead. Some farmers are now offering it for sale, often delivered. It is quite often advertised in the local paper at about £10 to £15 a bale, comparing favourably with hay prices.

One bulk food that should be mentioned before passing on to green food, is straw. Goats will often eat it in preference to poor hay, but it does not have a high food value on its own, and must be supplemented with grazing or other green food, or perhaps grass nuts. It is therefore suitable for feeding at night in summer, when the goats have been on lush grazing all day. In some districts baled pea haulm is available, which, if you can get it, is excellent.

CROPS TO GROW

If you have the land to spare, and the necessary machinery for cultivation, you may wish to grow some field crops suitable for goat feeding. As, in most districts, grass grows better than anything else during summer, you would be most likely to cultivate winter greens and roots. Apart from potatoes, which are not so well liked, any root crop is suitable, including swedes, stubble turnips, carrots and, probably the best of all, fodder beet. Unlike sheep,

38

goats are not usually grazed on these out in the field so they will have to be harvested, stored, cleaned and chopped before feeding, probably in troughs. Kale and cattle cabbages are also very useful, but will also have to be cut and carted, as goats are not normally prepared to wade into mud to get their food like cattle! If yours is only a small herd, where handfeeding of green plants and roots is not too difficult, there is a wide variety of crops you can make use of, especially from your own vegetable garden.

It is a good guideline to remember that goats can eat any of the plants that we eat, with a few exceptions. Rhubarb leaves and potato tops are poisonous, as well as tomatoes, which being of the same family as the latter, are suspect. Brassicas, which are all members of the cabbage family, should not be fed once they have really gone to seed, or in excessive amounts over long periods, especially when not mixed with plants of other families. The tops of beetroot, fodder beet and spinach beet should all be well wilted before feeding to reduce the oxalic acid content, but are then safe. Totally harmless and well liked are all pea and bean plants and pods, carrot tops, bolted lettuce and Chinese cabbages, as well as prunings from fruit bushes and trees.

One plant that is very easy to grow on a small scale and which is well worthwhile is Russian comfrey. Being a hybrid, it is not grown from seed but roots can often be obtained from friends, and these can be split and grown into new plants from small pieces. Providing that you do not let the plant dry out during its first summer, it will grow and proliferate, even if then neglected. However, if well cared for, weeded, manured and kept damp, it will grow at such a rate that you can cut it several times a year right down to the ground. Frequent cutting will encourage the greatest yield. Once established, Russian comfrey will never suffer in a drought as its roots go down very deep. Because of this, never plant it in the wrong place, because it is very difficult to eradicate later. It can thrive in any odd corner, tolerates shade and does particularly well along ditches and in wet patches where only rushes grow. It is higher in protein than any other green plant, with a good fibre content and an abundance of vitamins and minerals. If all that were not enough, it has extraordinary healing properties for cuts and wounds. The only disadvantage is that it dies down after the first frost, so some winter greens should be grown to fill the gap then.

WILD PLANTS

Apart from all these plants that you can grow especially for them, goats will eat a wide choice of the plants that grow whether you intend them to or not. I am referring of course to 'weeds', and this is where goats really come into their own as such wonderfully useful animals. They are capable of improving rough grassland and moorland grazing because of their liking for the less desirable species (from an agricultural point of view), and ability to encourage the growth of clover and grass. They relish most of the common garden and field weeds such as thistles, docks, dandelions, milk thistles, willowherb, fat hen, ground elder, hogweed and scores of others. As far as I know goats are the only species that will graze nettles fresh while they are still stinging. They appear to be unmoved by the irritant and it does not even seem to affect the tender skin of their udders. They like to decide for themselves when nettles are fit to eat and will often ignore them for weeks, then suddenly all descend upon them as if they had just discovered them. Tethered goats do not eat them as well as loose ones, possibly because they do not have this opportunity for self selection. However, all goats will eat them when they are cut and put in a rack, and they are particularly relished when dry and crisp. During a good summer you can dry a few for the winter when they are invaluable if you have a sick goat, as they are a very palatable source of the vitamins and minerals that goats need.

It has been a tradition for smaller goatkeepers to collect wild food from the hedgerows, but I feel that we should take care not to damage the disappearing vegetation, now that hedgerow plants are under such pressure from flail hedgetrimmers, sprays and car pollution. Try to use only the most common plants and shrubs that can stand frequent pruning. Hogweed is one such plant, which goats love and which can be cut frequently. Beware of the poisonous imported giant hogweed, which grows to an enormous height and is becoming more common. The safe native variety only grows to about 6ft (1.8m) maximum and is very common by roadsides.

Trees should always be treated with respect while cutting food and should not be hacked and torn. Willow, especially *Salix caprea* (goat willow), lives up to its name and can take any amount of pruning. It can be grown as a windbreak on damp land, being very easily cultivated from cuttings, or you could try one of the newer giant hybrids.

Although there are a number of safe plants from the flower garden, such as roses, many ornamental shrubs are dangerous. The worst include yew, laburnum, sumach, rhododendron, and related plants such as azaleas. It is best to avoid all evergreens except holly and ivy, which are positively good for goats. Of the wild plants there are not many which are both very deadly and common, and goats will avoid some, such as foxglove. Hemlock, dog's mercury, and deadly nightshade should be identified from a good plant book. Two plants which are both common and dangerous are ragwort and bracken. If your land is infested with either of these, it would be as well to get some advice, although bracken is eaten only rarely, usually during a severe shortage of grass. Ragwort is especially dangerous in hay. It is easily pulled up, so if you come across even one plant while walking in the field, pull it up at once and take it away for burning. Never leave it lying on the ground as it is more palatable when wilted. The British Goat Society produces a very cheap leaflet called 'Wild food for goats' listing many safe species as well as the poisonous ones to avoid.

CONCENTRATE FEEDING

The modern dairy goat, who is expected to produce far more milk than her wild counterpart, must also have more nutritious food added to her natural diet. However good the bulk food, she will need some more concentrated protein and energy as well, especially if a good winter milk supply is needed.

A great deal has been written about concentrates for goats, some of it very technical, some full of wild inaccuracies. I am going to avoid making hard and fast statements, because as I have said, goats are adaptable, thriving on many different systems and diets. In the past, before commercial goatkeeping became respectable, most well-bred, high-yielding goats were kept primarily for showing. As a result, each breeder had his own pet way of producing winners and high yields, and there is no doubt that there have been many top herds fed on unscientific, and apparently unbalanced, rations. Because this book is intended as a practical guide for low-cost production, milk must not be produced at an unreasonable cost in either time or money, and therefore my views on concentrate feeding may differ from those of other authors. I do feel however, that when you buy your first goats it is advisable to keep them on the same sort of regime and feed that they were used to, only gradually changing later if you wish.

Nowadays, there are many different goat mixes produced by all the main feed firms and many smaller ones, and I feel that the beginner cannot go far wrong in using one of these. The manufacturers have gone to a great deal of trouble in formulating the feeds so that they are balanced for milk production, and for this reason it is unwise to upset the balance by adding bran or oats. The only exception would be in order to reduce the protein content for feeding to non-milking goatlings. This protein is shown as a percentage on the ticket, where you will also find the oil content, which influences the energy value. Most goat mixtures have a protein level of between 14 and 17 per cent with some having a higher oil content than others. As a rule, a feed made by one of the well-known national firms, or a reliable local one, is likely to be of good quality. They have reputations to keep and the rivalry and competition is very intense. Most of them are aware of the health-food image of goats' milk and will use only the best-quality ingredients. Naturally one would be suspicious of a feed noticeably cheaper than other similar ones, as it is likely that the ingredients may be of poor quality.

Different feed values are needed at different times of the year and at the various stages of a goat's growth. A heavily milking goat being stall-fed, or without access to spring grass, should have around a 16 per cent mixture with a high energy value. The same animal on ample spring grass would be content with a 14 per cent feed, or even less. The protein level should be brought up to about 16 per cent by September and would remain the same if the goat is expected to milk on through the winter. A high protein diet is not needed so much during pregnancy, but the energy content must increase gradually towards kidding. This energy would normally be supplied by one of the good goat mixes, which could have a little cereal added at this stage, or by high energy dairy nuts or goat nuts.

Dairy Nuts

Cow dairy nuts are frequently scorned by other goatkeeping authors. One cannot help wondering if they have ever used them over a long period as we did before goat pellets were on the market. Apart from very cheap 'grazing nuts', dairy feeds are of good quality. I do not believe that they are full of rubbish, such as chicken manure, as some people claim, because both cows and goats enjoy them, and milk well. You cannot escape from the fact that virtually all of this country's cows' milk is produced with the aid of dairy nuts, and farmers are not known for wasting money on tons of rubbish! If you buy a very cheap make, you get what you pay for, but those made by reputable firms are a different matter.

Nut-type feeds are normally cheaper per ton than coarse feeds, and are easier to dispense from milking parlour hoppers if you are feeding in this way. There are now a few feed firms making proper goat nuts or pellets, and these are ideal, as the goats cannot pick out only the bits they like best as they do with coarse feeds. We use them all the time now as they are very convenient. There is one in the form of a small pellet, which can be used for the youngest kid up to the milkers. Being made by a Westcountry feed firm, they are not, unfortunately, available nationally. However Spillers now make a goat cube which is gradually becoming widely available.

Cereal Feeds

If you need to reduce the protein of a nut feed, you can either mix it with cereal, such as barley or oats, or add sugar-beet pellets. Cereal is also suitable for adding to a coarse feed for this purpose. To work out what protein level you are going to finish up with, you have to know what you begin with and mix accurately. For instance, oats are usually about 8.5 per cent protein, so if you add one part by weight to one part of goat mix at 17 per cent, you would have a finished mix of 12 per cent. It is always wise to work out such mixtures carefully by weight in this way, because guessing is so inaccurate. It is also important to use a measure whose capacity for a given feed is known, for rationing out food to the goats. Remember that nuts are heavy and look less in volume than cereals.

Some people prefer to mix their own feeds from various cereals and protein cakes available from merchants. You can certainly save money by doing this, especially if you are able to purchase barley or oats direct from a farmer. You may want to make use of a local source of organically grown cereal. However, it is important that you are certain of what you are doing, and that the final mixture will be balanced with all the elements that a goat needs. A proper goat vitamin and mineral mixture such as Caprivite should be added. If possible try to use a variety of cereals and oil cakes, not forgetting the high energy foods such as flaked maize and sugar-beet pulp. Oats are the traditional cereal used for goats, but there is nothing wrong with barley if it is not fed to excess. Oats are often fed whole, and goats certainly seem to like them that way, although, like all new foods, they should be introduced gradually.

Goat Nutrition, the makers of Caprivite, also make a high-protein mixture formulated for adding to cereal as a balancer, which makes mixing feeds at home far simpler for the beginner. Other firms make similar products under various trade names, and these grain balancers, as they are called, are particularly appropriate when you have grown the cereal yourself, as the finished mixture then works out at a very economical price.

It used to be said that goats should have a large proportion of bran in the mixture, but this is not so generally advocated now. Bran is very highly priced in relation to its feed value and the mineral content is very imbalanced, especially when fed with other cereals. Humans may benefit from the roughage it provides but goats are normally getting plenty of fibre from their natural diet. Animal feed cereals are not refined like those in human food, so there is no need to add more fibre unless it is in the form of a high feed value product like sugar-beet pulp, the by-product of the sugar refining industry.

Sugar-Beet Pulp
This is one feed we always like to use for our goats, as it is an excellent high-energy, highly digestible fibre food, can be fed in several different ways and is always well liked. It can either be used as part of a goat mixture, replacing some of the cereal, when it is likely to be in the shredded form, or as a separate feed during the day, or late at night. Many goatkeepers use it in this way, some giving it as a midday feed in winter, when the goats are in all day. It is most readily available during the late autumn and winter, with some merchants having stocks to carry them into the

spring. Unfortunately it is not always available during summer, when it would make an ideal combination with grass feeding. It is supplied in various forms, including dried shredded pulp, or compressed into a nut after being molassed. Because these nuts are rather large for goats, we prefer to use the pellets, which are about the size of a dairy nut.

A very common misconception that folk have, is that sugar beet must always be soaked in water for several hours before feeding. There is no harm whatever in feeding the nuts, pellets or pulp dry, and that is how the former two are designed to be given to ruminants, as opposed to horses who must *always* have it soaked. If they were intended to be soaked, the makers would hardly go to the trouble and expense of making nuts and pellets. As with all feeds, it should be introduced gradually, and water must be provided for the goats to drink after eating. This will result in a swelling of the food in the stomach, but I can assure you that the goat rrumen is very capacious and more than able to cope, providing it is not already overfull with lush grass, for instance. This is why we use it at midday in winter, when the goats are beginning to feel a little empty. I would feed a maximum of one pound of nuts or pellets at one time in these circumstances. If your goats prefer it soaked, then continue to give it in that way, but do not feel that you have to. The owners of large herds would find handling large amounts of wet pulp much more inconvenient than a bag of nuts. In some areas of the country mixed nuts can be obtained, often containing dried grass, which makes an excellent combination. Grass nuts are high in protein, but low in energy, thus balancing the sugar beet. They are made entirely from rapidly dried grass, usually without any additives, and so are a 'natural' concentrate for goats, who, unfortunately, do not always like them.

Quantity to Feed
It is very difficult in a book of this kind to be adamant about the quantity of concentrate to feed in any given situation, as so much depends upon the quality and availability of the bulk food and the stage of lactation or growth of the goats. Much more detailed information and tables of feed requirements and values can be found in some new scientific goat books, and from such bodies as the Goat Producers Association, or the Goat Veterinary Society. The following guidelines will give the goat the

basic essentials for fitness and reproduction, but the feeding of animals is largely a matter of common sense, and of observing their bodily condition.

A goat needs far more nutritious food at certain times of her life, the first six months being very important (see Chapter 8). If she is not mated during her first winter when about ten months old, thus becoming an unmated goatling, her needs will be much lower during the next months, especially if she is on good grazing. You may well find that dry goatlings like this need hardly any concentrate, but it is worth giving them just a taste, to keep them in the habit.

During the final two months of pregnancy, goats should be on an increasingly nutritious diet, with particular attention paid to the energy supplied. After kidding the amount of feed given is increased as the milk production rises. A goat yielding about 8–12 pt (4.5–7L) a day will need between 3 and 4lb (1.4 and 1.8kg) of concentrate. Once the production is established, you will be able to reduce the concentrates fed during spring and early summer if the grazing is good, without losing milk or the goats' condition. Goats who are milking through for a second summer need far less concentrate than their freshly kidded sisters, and can be at real risk of becoming too fat at this time. 1–2lb ($^1/_2$–1kg) of concentrate should be ample for them.

All goats who are expected to milk on well into the winter or beyond should have an increase in both quantity and quality at about September. There is always a certain decline in yield at that time of year, but it can be minimized by good feeding before the goats have all but dried up. This regime applies to goats on ample grazing or adequate cut green food, but if stall-feeding, you would almost certainly have to use more concentrates at times. Do, however, carefully watch those unmated goatlings and run-through goats and never allow them to become fat.

If you have young goats that were mated in their first winter to kid when about fourteen to eighteen months old, they will need better feeding all the time they are still growing. In practice, this is until about the end of the summer following the one in which they first kidded, when they are about twenty-eight months old. In the matter of goat feeding, there is no substitute for experience, and it is often a matter of trying different combinations until you find what your goats do best on.

WATER AND MINERALS

I have already mentioned water briefly in Chapter 2. A milking animal needs good access to water or succulent food, as milk is largely water. Sometimes even when a goat is milking well, you may feel that she is not drinking enough, especially if she is on wet grass. Goats are creatures who are not naturally inclined to drink a lot, often hardly touching their buckets when they are not milking, but they should be encouraged to drink for maximum milk production. The water must be changed frequently and the buckets kept clean, with field tanks also being brushed out regularly. Some goatkeepers add extras to their goats' water, such as salt or molasses, but ours prefer it plain. Others give warm water, and this can certainly aid intake. It is a little impractical and expensive for commercial herds though, and we only give warm water to freshly kidded goats in very cold weather. Rainwater collected in tanks from farm roofs seems to be preferred to tap water, and it is also free if you are on a water meter.

Another essential ingredient of the diet is salt. The simplest way to provide for this is by means of a salt and mineral lick, placed either in the yard where they all have access, or hung between each pair of pens. Although minerals are included in these licks, many people feel that they are insufficient for the mineral-hungry goat and add some to their feed. As previously mentioned, it is important to do this when mixing your own feed, but less so if using a proper goat mix as they will have already been included.

In some parts of the country there are mineral deficiencies in the soil and it is as well to talk to your vet about this if you are worried. He may wish to test a few blood samples to see if there are any imbalances. I feel that too many inexperienced goatkeepers add certain minerals to the feed without really knowing what they are doing, thereby unbalancing other minerals. Apart from the problem of specific local deficiencies, the best way to ensure a good balance is to provide pasture and other bulk food with as wide a variety of 'herbs' or weeds as possible. This is difficult when you buy in all your hay and this is where easily grown plants like nettles and comfrey are so useful. There is a gradual movement back towards mixed pastures with many different plants, and this is a very good thing for the health of all stock.

47

CHAPTER FIVE

MILKING AND THE DAILY ROUTINE

It hardly needs saying that your goats are going to need milking every day, twice a day, come rain or shine. The way that you intend organising this necessary routine is something to consider when planning your enterprise. First of all there is a decision to make between hand or machine milking. Of course, if you are beginning with a large number of goats in milk, you would be going for machine milking right away. If, like so many people, you start the enterprise in a very small way, with fewer than ten goats, hand milking has a number of advantages, the main one being that the equipment and facilities needed are very much easier and cheaper to set up than a milking parlour. Basically all you need is a goat, a bucket and your hands! Naturally, it is not quite as simple as that, especially when producing milk for human consumption, when hygiene is so important.

LEARNING TO HAND MILK

Even if you are planning a large herd, I would suggest that any would-be goatkeeper begins by learning to hand milk. It is such a useful skill to have, quickly learnt, and invaluable for emergencies such as power cuts, goats with badly torn teats, or those with mastitis. It is preferable to learn from an experienced goat milker, rather than attempting to teach oneself, practising on a cow, or having instruction from someone used only to cows. In these cases it would be the goats who suffer. People often pretend to milk animals on the television, and invariably use a downward, pulling motion, which is quite wrong. Cow milkers also sometimes use this technique, or a stripping motion with finger and thumb down the teat; something that most goats dislike. This is because the goats' teats are much softer and more tender than those of cows and less pressure is needed to squeeze the milk out.

Try to find a suitable goatkeeper (perhaps through your local goat club), and ask if she will teach you on a—hopefully—placid, mature goat. If you are buying milking stock from a breeder, she would probably insist on a lesson if you are unfamiliar with goats. Almost all goats are quiet to milk when handled correctly, but even the most patient of animals will rebel if her teats are pulled!

The correct action is almost impossible to convey by the printed word, but it could be described as being like trying to move a bubble of air from one end of a partly deflated balloon to the other with the fingers of one hand. The aim is to trap the milk in the teat and press it out, while keeping the top end of the teat compressed to prevent the milk going back up again. It is more of a squeeze or press than a pull. It requires more pressure than you think, but if the goat is happy and the milk is coming out, then you have mastered the action. Everybody finds it difficult at first, especially aiming at the bucket, and right-handed people find using their left hand more difficult and vice versa. Once you have the action though, you will only improve and speed comes with long practice. I have never taught anyone who failed to learn, but some are quicker than others.

It is essential to convince the goat that you know what you are doing, however unsure you feel; she will be far less likely to play up if you approach her with confidence. Although experienced goatkeepers do not always tie their goats by the collar, I think it is wise. Ideally you need a milking bench to stand the goat on, as she will be easier to control if she is higher up. Sit on the edge of the bench and, if necessary, lean into her side to restrict movement. The bench should always be close against a wall, to prevent her moving away from you. It may seem obvious, but always milk with both hands, even if it is difficult at first, or one hand will become lazy and never learn.

Personally I do not feed goats while they are being milked, as I have always found that they learn to stand still more easily when chewing the cud. It is a natural reaction to cud while suckling a kid; cudding is conducive to tranquillity, and failure to cud at milking can be the first indication that something is amiss. One of the snags of feeding while milking is that she will have to continue to occupy the bench until she has finished, or, on the other hand, she will want to be off as soon as the food is gone, whether or not milking is completed.

HYGIENIC MILKING

When producing milk for sale, goats should never be milked in their pens amongst all the dung and straw, but should be taken to a small clean, washable area equipped with the milking bench. Most goats learn to jump onto a raised platform very quickly and are then secured by the collar. I do not like the more complicated type of stand that holds the goat by means of a yoke locked around the neck. I find that goats are so amenable to milking that very little restraint is needed. A simple spring-hook attached to the wall at the right height to clip to the collar is enough. If your goats do not wear collars, a short length of chain stapled to the wall will suffice, to loop and fasten round the neck.

The only receptacle that should really be used for commercial milking is a proper stainless-steel milking pail. These are made in a suitable goat size and are very long lasting, simple to clean and sterilise, and well worth the cost. If you have to use something else temporarily, it must be an article made for food use, and not a coloured plastic household bucket.

After having washed her hands and donned a clean overall, the milker should first wipe the udder. Strictly speaking this is often considered unnecessary for the typically clean goat, but most people do it as a routine. Handling the udder also encourages the let-down of milk. Many goatkeepers now use the modern impregnated teat wipes, and others an udder cloth soaked in a suitable solution. Udder washing liquids are available from agricultural stores, but some people use a disinfectant like Capriclense. Hypochlorite is not suitable as it irritates the skin. Udder cream can be used either before or after milking if the skin feels rough or chapped. It does wonders for your hands too!

The first few squirts of milk are discarded or kept for the farm cats. If you use a proper strip-cup, with a black disc in the lip, you can see any clots in the milk which could indicate mastitis. This is considered an early-warning system, but in my experience, goats with mastitis tend to have clots at the end of milking rather than the beginning. Once the main amount of milk has been drawn and the flow starts to lessen, massage the udder downwards and more will come. Do this several more times until the flow ceases.

You should aim to take virtually every drop from the udder at each milking, as the quantity will decrease if you fail to do this.

MACHINE MILKING

Larger commercial herds will go straight for machine milking. I will refer again to milking parlours and dairies in Chapter 11, covering some of the regulations involved. For now it is enough to say that unless you have a herd of about fifty or more, it is by no means essential to have a purpose-built milking parlour. Small herds only need a place where hygienic milking can be carried out with a small bucket-unit milking machine. Nowadays, a number of well-known milking machine firms supply goat milkers and most can offer anything from a single bucket milker, right up to a proper milking parlour with a barrier to hold the goats' heads, several units milking at once, and a bulk tank for the milk. In such parlours the goats are normally raised up so that the operator has them at more or less eye level. They are usually fed while milked in this way, and food dispensers are an integral part. I do feel that you lose out a little on the close relationship possible between milker and goats when only seeing the back end and udder of each animal.

We use a two-goat bucket unit consisting of a combination of new goat milking parts, and second-hand cow equipment, such as the actual buckets. In our case the goats are milked from the side as they would be by hand, but you can choose goat clusters which milk either from the side or rear, between the legs. Goats who are used to hand milking take more easily to the former.

To machine milk, wash or wipe the goat's udder as described above, discard the first few squirts of milk and attach the teat cups to begin milking. Watch carefully, so that you can take off the cluster the moment she is milked. All milking machines have a glass or other transparent part so that you can see when the milk flow has stopped. Transparent silicone rubber teat-cup liners are very good in this respect, as it is most important never to leave them on too long, and in fact we usually remove the cluster when the main flow has ceased and milk the final strippings by hand. Opinions vary about whether hand stripping is a good practice or not, but it suits our goats. It also keeps them used to hand milking, and they are not upset by being hand milked on occasions.

After milking, all equipment and pipes should be rinsed, washed and sterilised according to the manufacturer's instructions. Needless to say, this must not be skimped, and it would be wise to get some detailed instruction on all machine-milking matters before you begin. If you have a well-known firm to install your parlour and tank you will find that they are all now knowledgeable about goat milking and will give valuable advice. It is also important, if you are intending to have a small bucket unit, to find someone to install it who really knows the difference between cow and goat milking. The vacuum for goats is lower and the pulsation different. If you are making use of second-hand equipment, it is essential that you get these details right, or mastitis could result. I am certain that whatever else is second hand, the pulsator should be bought new, from a firm such as Fullwood and Bland who make ones for goats (see Useful Addresses, page 166) and I would also advise using a goat cluster. With any second-hand equipment new rubbers and liners will be needed, and in any case cow clusters have four teat cups and are much too heavy for goats. One disadvantage of some of the small bucket unit milkers is that the motor (which is usually electric, but can be petrol) is joined to the bucket part, which means that it is in close proximity to where you are working. Personally, I find milking a very peaceful occupation and do not like a noisy motor and pump working near me. I doubt if the goats appreciate it either, so we house our motor in the adjoining building with the vacuum brought into the milking area by means of a pipe.

COOLING THE MILK

Immediately after milking, the milk must be strained and cooled. This is essential for all milk, however produced, although if you have a milking parlour, the milk probably passes directly into a bulk tank, where cooling is begun at once. Those who hand milk, or use the small milking machine, must carry the milk to the dairy, pour it through a strainer with a milk filter in place at the base, and begin cooling. For relatively small quantities of milk, goat equipment firms sell a strainer for fitting over the gallon-sized cans, and larger ones for full-sized churns can also be obtained. These are usually made of stainless steel, aluminium, or hard white, dairy quality plastic. Churns and cans of various sizes and all similar equipment, such as filter papers etc, are easily obtained by post or from agents of the many goat equipment firms. If you are living on a farm where cows were once kept, there may be equipment about that can be utilised if in good enough condition.

You may be surprised to hear that improper cooling is nearly always the cause of the unpleasant goats' milk that too many people still sell to the public. It is only rarely caused by the common reasons given, such as 'she ate something strong', 'the male goat was in the building', or even 'the goat is in season'. There is a belief understandably held by the public, that goats' milk is always 'strong' and goaty. Lack of proper cooling is the most certain way to develop that goaty taste. When it is kept at too warm a temperature for any length of time, the fats break down into different components which causes this goatiness. It has nothing to do with dirt bacteria either, or the milk going off, but it is a property that anyone producing milk for sale must be aware of. I believe cows' milk can break down in a similar way, but the balance of fatty acids is different, producing a more cheesey flavour instead. If goats' milk is cooled rapidly to at least tap-water

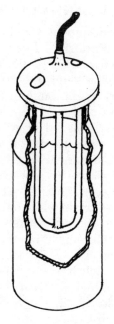

An in-churn milk cooler

temperature, and then stored under refrigeration, or frozen at once, the flavour will not develop at all. The colder the milk is kept, the longer it will keep sweet.

Placing the warm milk straight in the fridge will not do either; before the advent of refrigerated bulk tanks which gently move the milk, all cooling was done with the aid of running cold water, which is still just as effective, especially for a few gallons per milking session. Having strained the milk into a suitable-sized can, stand it in a bucket of water with the tap running slowly. If you are on a meter, or have a limited supply, this wasteage can often be collected for washing down and goat drinking. Once the temperature of the milk is as low as the water, it should be placed in the fridge or frozen. It should never be left about at room temperature unless only destined for animal consumption. For quantities of milk too great for this simple method, and too small for a bulk tank, old-fashioned cow churns are best, which can be fitted with an in-churn cooler which also works on the water cooling principle, but more efficiently.

WASHING AND STERILISING

After milking all the equipment should be cleaned and sterilised. Milking parlour pipes should be washed according to the manufacturer's instructions. Small bucket units are normally washed through with dairy detergent/steriliser twice a day, and periodically taken apart for thorough brushing and cleaning.

All buckets, strainers and cans should be rinsed in cold or slightly tepid water first, washed in very hot water containing dairy detergent and then sterilised. It is very rare these days for small producers to have steam chests and virtually everyone uses a chemical like dairy hypochlorite. Also available are iodine-based ones such as Capriclense, which are most suitable for aluminium and other metals, but will stain white dairy plastic. Personally, I like the clean smell of hypochlorite, which has a good deodorizing effect and will also bleach. It is however, really only suitable for plastic or stainless steel, and will damage aluminium if used too strong, or the items are left immersed too long. It is safe to dip aluminium cans for the required two minutes to sterilise, but they will darken and lose their shine. Stainless steel is by far the best material for dairy equipment, but many people have to use something cheaper to begin with. The cost of stainless-steel milk cans, for instance, is very high. Plastic is not ideal because of the difficulty of cleaning it properly, but it is necessary for some things, like cheese moulds and mats, which should be left to soak in the hypochlorite for as long as possible. Once taken out, all equipment should be stored upside down to drain and not dried with a cloth.

THE GOATS' DAILY ROUTINE

Unless they were fed during milking, most goats are given their concentrates immediately after milking. Not counting their lunchtime sugar beet, ours have two feeds per day, and have half in the morning and half after the afternoon milking. As soon as possible after milking, most goats are let out into the field, or if it is winter, they have a rack of silage or hay, about half their daily ration. Stall-fed herds are often given green food at this time of day.

If you are relying on electric fencing, it is essential to check periodically that it is working properly. Some fencer units have an indicator light, or you can use one of the light-up line testers. Walking round the electric fencing is a very pleasant job on a fine day, and you can observe your goats as you go. They should never just be put out and ignored all day, as goats can break out of fields, or get their heads caught in wire. Observation is vital if they are tethered, chains can so easily tangle, or the goats may pull up their stakes and break loose. They are very much at the mercy of the weather, and you may wish to dress them in the coats referred to in Chapter 3. Otherwise, during winter, they are better off indoors unless they have access to shelter. The feed value of natural vegetation in winter is so low that they lose more energy trying to keep warm than they gain by grazing. Because of the goat's adaptability, they soon become accustomed to their winter-time routine of being in all day. Ideally at this time, they should have a feed at midday to break up the day. This can either be sugar-beet nuts, or roots, green food or grass nuts.

Later in the day during summer, goats who have been out in the fields will have to be brought in .This is normally no problem, even if you have a very large herd, as goats are good at telling the time, and know when they should move towards the gate. It does help to have a good collie dog, in case they should be reluctant. We use two different collies on our herd, one completely untrained, but who knows where the goats are supposed to head for and is

very good at chasing up wanderers. The other, a well-bred registered Border Collie bitch, is more the true sheep dog type and
is excellent at actually rounding them up and keeping them in a
bunch. She is not quite as good at heading off a really awkward
goat as the other dog, as unlike her she will not bark. Using a dog
gently does save time, especially if you are in a hurry, although
there is nothing that will bring a herd of goats in faster than a
really heavy downpour. This is not always easy to arrange at the
right time though!

After the afternoon milking, the procedure with the milk is the
same as the morning, the goats are fed again and the racks filled
up. The times at which you milk can be arranged to suit your
circumstances, especially if you have children to see to or other
commitments. Once you have decided on your milking times, you
should adhere to them, and they should be as near twelve hours
apart as possible, although in practice, most herds have a longer
interval at night.

If you have reliable fencing and a suitably situated goathouse,
goats can be left out at night in the summer, when they come and
go at will. However, most people sleep more soundly in their beds
in the knowledge that their goats are safe inside out of harm's way.

OTHER ROUTINE TASKS

Grooming
There are a number of jobs that need to be done every now
and then, but do not have to be attended to daily. These include
the care of the goats' skin, hair and feet. People often ask about
grooming and whether goats should be brushed as a routine like
horses. There is no hard and fast rule, although in the case of large
commercial herds, the time involved would preclude it. I would
say, that unless your goats are always stall-fed, and you are prepared to rug them if necessary, you should only groom them during
late spring and summer, and stop again before the winter. Goats
who have to put up with the vagaries of the British climate need
all the coat they can grow, although modern dairy goats normally
only carry a fine sleek coat. Breeds like the old English and some
Toggenburgs will develop a fine woolly undercoat, which is in fact
cashmere, one of the most valuable fibres. Before you get excited
and begin counting the money, housed dairy goats produce very
little indeed! In order to produce any marketable quantity you

need a substantial herd of feral, 'wild' goats or first cross Angoras (see Chapter 11).

At the end of the winter, goats usually look very untidy, the cashmere will be coming out as a grey fluff, and they may have begun to moult their hair. Should you want to show them during the summer, or even if you just feel you would prefer them to look less disreputable, you can now begin to brush, encouraging the old hair to come out. Do not be tempted to do this too early if your goats are going to be out a great deal in spring. In colder districts it is advisable to wait until they start to moult naturally, which can be as late as mid-summer. Some goats moult in a very dramatic manner, losing almost all their hair at once. This looks dreadful, but only occasionally is it caused by a hormone or mineral imbalance. If the goat is well otherwise the new hair will re-grow quickly. Fairly vigorous brushing, even of the bare skin, will encourage the new, fine hair, and remove the unpleasant scurf which may also be present.

Scurfy skin and hair loss can be an indication of lice, which are quite common in winter, even in the best of herds. Goats should never be allowed to become heavily infested as these parasites will drag a goat right down in condition. On a warm spring day, an animal shampoo can be used; otherwise, dust the goat all over with a farm louse powder. There are other products available if you have a stubborn problem with lice; see Chapter 9.

Foot Trimming
Another routine task that must not be neglected is foot trimming. The goat was designed for running about on rocky and other abrasive surfaces, and rarely inhabits damp grassland. As a consequence, in the domestic situation, their hooves grow too fast, and never wear down. Overgrown feet, combined with our damp, soft, British grassland, or deep litter bedding, can spell disaster unless the feet are looked at frequently, and trimmed. Goats kept on concrete for part of the day will be better off, but there is no escaping regular foot trimming.

It is usually suggested that goats' feet should be trimmed once a month, but this can be impossible in a farm herd. To be practical, one should aim to trim goats' feet *before* they become lame, or the feet are deformed, or develop foot rot. While milking, you can easily take note of any goat whose feet need attention, and attend to her later, perhaps after they have come in off grass, when the horn will have softened a little in the damp and will be easier to cut.

Foot trimming, like milking, is another of those things which really needs a practical demonstration, and in this respect, your local club may organise open days at breeders' premises, where you can see the technique at first hand. Dairy goats are not normally upended like sheep to have this done, one reason being that they do not sit placidly in this position, but will always struggle to get up. Stress is something to be avoided always, and so the usual practice is to lift one foot at a time like shoeing a horse. Most goats are fairly co-operative about having their front hooves trimmed, but less so with the rear. It helps if you have an assistant to hold the goat firmly by the collar. If you are alone, the same effect can be had by tying her alongside a wall, while you work on the legs on one side and then turn her round to do the other two.

The outside of the hoof is like a toe nail, always growing, and the goat is, in effect, walking on the points of its toes. If you did not cut your toe nails at all and walked in this manner, the nail would bend over and form a flap. This is what happens in the goat, the surplus horn grows under the sole, trapping the dirt in the flap and setting up a rot, if neglected. This flap must be trimmed right off and the appropriate tool for this is a pair of proper foot shears as made for sheep. Some people prefer a sharp knife and others flat-bladed secateurs, but nothing is quite as effective, and simple to use, as the foot shears. A proper hoof knife is also useful for levelling off after the greater part of the surplus has been removed, and also for flattening the rubbery heel at the back, although this can be done with the shears alone. It is important, when unused to foot trimming, to only take off a little at a time. If used to sheep, you will see that goats usually have far more horn to take off. Most goats have white horn, making it easy to see when the pink of the quick is showing. Stop cutting as soon as you see this pink tinge, but do not panic if you make the foot bleed, just wash well and spray with a suitable antiseptic spray. Strong pressure with a finger will normally stop bleeding.

If you buy goats from a good home, the seller will often demonstrate foot trimming for you at the time. In any case, it is usual to attend to a goat's feet prior to selling her.

BEDDING

Apart from wet fields, there is nothing more conducive to foot trouble than wet, soggy bedding, so always keep a good dry layer on the top if using deep litter. This bedding will only have to be cleaned out when it becomes too high, or too wet. Goats seem to like the deep litter system, especially in winter when it provides the original under-floor heating. If preferred, goats can be cleaned out every day, like horses, but this is more wasteful of straw, because goats should not have to lie on only a thin layer over concrete. They do however enjoy lying on wood, so daily cleaning out could be combined with a raised wooded sleeping bench like a pallet. Straw is the most usual bedding, barley considered the best, with oat or wheat usually cheaper. Wood shavings or forest bark can be used and these materials make a good base for the bottom layer of the bed in winter. Some people use poor hay which is not fit for feeding, but this can be risky, as the moulds which make bad hay dangerous to feed are still present for the goats to breathe in. Hay bedding also tends to smell more than straw, and is more difficult to muck out with a fork later. It is impossible though to prevent goats from wasting their best feeding hay, as some is bound to finish up on the floor, resulting, inevitably, in a mixed hay and straw bed.

Some farmers may consider slatted floors which are often used in intensive livestock systems to avoid the use of straw. Personally I do not think that goats would be particularly comfortable or clean on this type of floor, and I do not know of anyone who uses it. In order to keep your herd sweet and clean, with sound feet, you cannot skimp on bedding, and those living in straw-growing areas of the country have a great advantage in this respect. The manure from this deep litter is invaluable, and I will refer to it again in Chapter 12.

CHAPTER SIX

BREEDS AND BREEDING

There is a distinction between mating goats in order that they should produce milk, and breeding them for improvement of the youngstock. Very few goatkeepers, whether commercial or not, wish to do what many cow dairy farmers do, which is to buy in all their replacement milkers without rearing any from their own stock. In any case, it is difficult to do this with goats, as it can be all but impossible to go and buy a group of white milkers, all freshly kidded, whereas the ordinary dairy farmer can go to market or to a dealer, and buy as many freshly calved Friesians as he needs. This means that when goatkeepers mate their milkers, they are doing so not only to produce milk, but also to breed a female kid who will be a potential improvement on her dam. You would not necessarily want to do this with all your goats, as you may need only a few replacements each year. The kids from other dams may be intended for sale, or meat, or even to be put down at birth. It goes without saying, that any kid intended for future milk production, either in your herd or someone else's, should be sired by a good 'milky' male. Mating a goat is of course necessary to get her in kid, but in order to breed better animals all the time, a great deal of thought needs to go into this natural process.

CHOOSING A BREED

Firstly, you will have to decide what breed of goat you want. In Chapter 1, I touched on the matter of pedigree goats as being generally superior. If you have begun with pedigree British Saanens, for instance, the chances are that you will want to stay with that breed, so the decision is simple. If, like many beginners, you have had to buy a few goats here and there, some registered, some not, and some of mixed breeding, you can decide what breed of male to use. Although nothing looks better than a whole herd of the

60

same breed or colour together on a farm, it is difficult for many of us to make up our minds to stick to one breed. Some commercial herds have British Saanens for quantity of milk, with a few Anglo Nubians for better quality milk for cheese or yogurt.

The two original Swiss breeds that were imported into this country at the end of the last century are the TOGGENBURG and the SAANEN. People advertising goats for sale have a tendency to call any white goat a Sannen and any brown one a Toggenburg, but unless they are registered in the appropriate section of the Herd Book, and have the card to prove it, goats should be described as Saanen or Toggenburg type. Neither of these two breeds can be graded up, but have to be pure-bred all the way.

Toggenburg

Toggenburgs are fairly small attractive goats, brown in colour, most usually of a pale shade, and sometimes having a fringe of long blond hair on the back and legs. All coloured Swiss-type goats have the same distinctive white stripes on the face and white on the legs and around the tail. A typical Toggenburg is of a 'milky' shape, with a long fine neck with a pretty head, deep body and short legs. They tend to have round udders with rather small teats admirably suited to machine milking. Being hardy goats of the true mountain type, they are good foragers and rangers and probably would not thrive as well under intensive conditions.

Saanen and British Saanen

The Saanen breed is probably the one most often associated with commercial herds as they are very placid goats, and heavy milkers. However, nearly all white goats of this type are British Saanen, based on Swiss Saanen blood which has been crossed and improved in Britain for many years. Pure Saanens are not easy to distinguish from their British cousins, only being perhaps a little smaller and finer boned. The difference is so slight as to be of little concern to a commercial goatkeeper. Either of the white breeds is ideally suited to intensive indoor herds, although they do equally well on good grass pasture. They are the easiest type to buy and probably have the best blood lines for milk production, capable of yields as high as 500 gallons a year when given individual attention in a show herd. 200 to 300 gallons is a more typical annual yield for commercial goats. They have been exported all over the world, and most of the goatkeeping countries such as the USA, Australia, New Zealand and South Africa have goats bred from British pedigree stock.

A specimen of either breed should be fine coated, pure white with only black skin spots permitted. She should have a long fine neck, feminine head, strong widely spaced hind legs, and a well-attached udder with small to medium teats. A common fault in unregistered white goats can be an unwieldy udder with large bulbous teats.

British Toggenburg

The British Toggenburg is not quite like its Swiss counterpart, although individuals with a high proportion of the original Toggenburg blood may look very like that breed in appearance. British Toggenburgs are usually bigger and taller, often darker in colour and are usually heavier milkers. The best ones are as good as the best British Saanens, but they are not quite so numerous. Non-pedigree brown goats can be very variable, some as good as the pedigree ones while others are very small, weedy 'scrubgoats'. We find that British Toggenburgs make good commercial goats for an outdoor life and are suited to milking through the winter and running on for a second year. They tend to be livelier than white goats and therefore sometimes need higher fences to contain them.

British Alpine

Possibly the worst goat for jumping out is the British Alpine, often having very long legs. They are an entirely made-up breed, produced in Britain from goats of mixed blood, but because they have the white Swiss markings, they were named the British Alpine, although they have never been near the Alps. As they are a shiny black and white they are very striking goats, tall and rangy with a bright, intelligent look about them. Good specimens can be few and far between, because, unlike the more fortunate British Saanen and British Toggenburg breeders, Alpine owners have no original pure breed to go back to for fresh blood. Some British Alpines have ugly, unwieldy udders which are unsuited to machine milking. This is a pity, because these goats are often the ones with good yields. Sometimes, in improving the udder shape, this yield declines, and I do not think they make ideal commercial goats. Some strains are also difficult to keep in good condition, so that they are inclined to look thin. This is not necessarily bad for the goat, but it makes the owner feel uncomfortable, and persuades her to feed more concentrates, thus making these goats less of a profitable type than the ones who are naturally better covered.

Anglo Nubian

The Anglo Nubian goat is an entirely different animal from the breeds based on European types. Its ancestors were desert goats from Egypt and India, and were thought to have come to this country by working their passage as milk providers on ships carrying service mens' families. They have a very distinctive appearance with long pendulous ears, roman noses and silky coats. Although they are intended to be large goats with long legs, not all of them fit this description, and some who are not of the best families are rather small.

Their attractive coats make them particularly noticeable, as they can be any colour or pattern at all, often being mottled or patchy. The most common colour is a roan or tan, with black legs, face and stripe along the back, but they can be anything from all black, to all white, and you never know what colour the kids are going to be. Naturally, these pretty goats must have one or two disadvantages, the worst being a tendency in many lines to dry up early in the autumn. Because of this, most require to be mated every year and will not run through readily. Their milk yield is generally lower than that of the Swiss goats, but they often have a much higher butterfat and protein content, making the milk ideal for cheese and yogurt making. They are not really suited to tethering and are probably not quite as hardy as other breeds. They are, however quite suitable for stall-feeding systems, having a tendency towards laziness.

THE GRADING-UP SYSTEM

Before I move on to the less common breeds, I must say a little about what are actually the most numerous of registered goats, the British. Because goats are kept primarily for milk, the British Goat Society allows cross breeding and up-grading of non-pedigree stock, and provides the British section of the Herd Book especially for them. This breed can either be the result of crossing two full pedigree breeds, or the descendant of an unregistered goat, moving up the grading system. Their appearance is often just like that of a breed type, especially if there is a high proportion of one particular breed in the family. Anglo Nubian goats crossed with others, usually produce kids which look halfway between the two breeds. Many of the best goats in the country are in the British section, and it is to the credit of the BGS for not bowing to the pressure of some perfectionists who would do away with these 'mongrels'. I prefer to think of them as farm hybrids, and as such they are of equal value to the pure-bred goats.

The BGS grading-up system is somewhat complicated for the uninitiated, but it becomes easier once you have bred and graded up a few yourself. Simplified, the rules are as follows: when an unregistered female goat is served by a pedigree male of any breed, the female kids can be registered in the Supplementary Register. When they grow up and are mated, the resulting female kids can go into the Foundation Book. When an FB goat kids, her daughters are entered in the British section. Each generation afterwards is moved up one stage, and providing that the right breed of male is used, after two more stages your goats will be in one of the pedigree breed sections. Male goats can only be registered once their mothers have reached the British section, and therefore should not be used for stud before this stage.

LESS COMMON BREEDS

There are a few other breeds which are not included in this grading system, some having special sections of their own, such as the Golden and English Guernsey, and others such as the Old English which are not recognised at all by the BGS.

Golden Guernseys are not normally kept for commercial purposes, being rather small and not noticeably heavy milkers. They are bred only from goats imported from the Channel Islands and are small dainty goats with coats varying from cream to dark auburn. Although they make ideal goats for family milkers, I do not know of anyone keeping a large herd on a commercial basis. They have a close relative, the English Guernsey, which has some Saanen or British Saanen blood to improve the milk yield. If you are interested in either of these breeds, it is important to contact a proper breeder, as many unregistered gold-colour goats are sold these days as Golden Guernseys.

The unrecognised Old English cannot go unmentioned. Owners in Scotland and Wales would probably prefer them to be called the British Native as they are the nearest domestic goat we have to those kept by crofters and cottagers in the past. These goats were presumed to have died out after the importation and development of the much heavier milking foreign breeds, but their colour type at least still exists. It is a matter of opinion whether the goats now registered with the English Goat Breeders Asssociation are really the same breed as the original, or an improved modern version. Personally, I do not think it matters; the breed can be ideal for the smallholder keeping goats to milk as naturally as possible. They are ideally suited to free-range scrub browsing and organic, low-input farming, and as such I think they have a future, whatever the controversy over their past. The most usual colour is russet, fawn or roan with a black dorsal stripe, not unlike the Anglo Nubian. There the resemblance ends for they have prick ears, very deep bodies and short legs. Some goats of this colour and type are registered in the lower grades of the BGS Herd Book, as recognised breed colour does not matter at this stage and a few registered males, usually BT type, will throw kids of this colour.

There are four other types of goat in Britain, three of which I will refer to in more detail in Chapter 11. These are the Angora—the Cashmere goat, and the wild, or more correctly 'feral' goat which is now being kept for cashmere fibre and meat. I only refer in passing to the Pygmy because this type is normally kept only as a non-breeding pet or an attraction in country parks and does not really come within the scope of this book. Although I am concentrating mainly on the dairy goat, the growing number of people keeping fibre-producing goats on a farm scale means that they are very much in the field of profitable goatkeeping (see Chapter 11).

CHOOSING A GOOD MALE

Having decided what breed or breeds of goat to keep it is necessary to have them served by the best male that you can buy or use. It is normal for larger goat farmers to keep their own males on the premises, but if you are just beginning and have fewer than ten goats to serve, it would pay you to use a good male at public stud. All local goat societies have a list of stud males in your area, but if you use one that is just advertised in the newspaper, make sure that he is a properly bred, registered male and ask to see his pedigree. I must repeat, that unless you are culling all kids at birth, it is just not worth using an unregistered male. The resulting female kids will be worth considerably less, you will know nothing about milk yields of his female relations and he may even be carrying serious faults like double teats. There is no guarantee that by using a pedigree male you are certain to improve your stock, but you have a much better chance of doing so. This applies even if you decide not to register the replacements for your herd, because the goat pedigree system is all connected with milk yields. The BGS has a system of awards and distinguishing marks which prove that at least a goat has a capability for a good yield. Some males known as Sires of Merit have fathered daughters who have won these milking awards. Although there is no progeny testing scheme such as that in the cattle world at present, the BGS awards are the best we have for the time being. People who keep stud males are usually dedicated breeders, striving to improve all the time, and will select a male to pass on good points like udder and teat shape, body depth, shape of hind legs, longevity of relatives, as well as less important show points such as the absence or presence of tassels. (These are the fleshy wattles hanging from some goats' necks; they have no significance or purpose, but are not supposed to be present in Anglo Nubians.)

Even when you are intending to rear the offspring for meat, it is worth using one of the cheaper pedigree males; the resulting kids will often have a faster growth rate than the true 'scrub'. Owners of stud males who keep more than one sometimes have one that is particularly suitable for the purpose. Angora males are also used for crossing with dairy goats for meat kid production.

Stud fees vary a great deal, but you are likely to pay between £7 and £15, or much more for the services of an Angora. For this sum you will have access to some of the best blood lines available to up-grade your herd. If you have more than ten females, you may wish to keep a male of your own, and should try to obtain the best you can afford. When you are more experienced, you may want to keep one from your own best line, but until then, it is easier to make use of someone else's knowledge of goat breeding and buy one, possibly from a milk-recorded herd. I would not suggest buying a male whose dam has only showing awards and nothing much in the milking competitions, as this would be far less suitable for a commercial herd. An alternative would be to buy a registered kid from a well-established commercial herd, where the goats have been purpose bred for a number of years.

HOUSING FOR MALE GOATS

If rearing a male kid, or indeed acquiring an adult, you will have to provide him with separate accommodation from the females. Not only do males have a very clinging and unpleasant smell, which is much worse in the breeding season, but they are very precocious as kids, and the wrong goat can so easily be served. A male kid should certainly not be in a pen with females from about three months of age, and you may well see that he is annoying and mounting them much sooner. In that case the separation should be made at once. He can stay with a castrated meat companion for a while, but eventually at about five or six months, he must move into his adult quarters. If only one male is kept, he will not feel so lonely if other stock such as pigs or cattle can be housed nearby for him to see. If two males are kept in adjoining pens, the division between them needs to be very strong, as a great deal of butting will go on during the breeding season. At other times of the year, males, especially when young, or already used to each other, can run together.

When planning the construction of a house for your first male goat, do visit a few herds where males are kept, to see just how strong and heavy they become when fully mature. The strength of the divisions and gates really needs to be as adequate as for cattle or ponies, as male goats can be very destructive. It is a great help if all the feeding can be done without entering the pen, and a concrete exercise yard for his sole use is very useful. Not all smallholders will be able to provide the perfect accommodation at once, but the male should be allowed as much space as possible, because he will need to be inside a great deal of the time.

The reason for feeding your male from outside the pen is not only because males can be very aggressive, but because of the smell problem. The scent of male goat is notorious and the public is only too ready to attribute it to all goats. If you are selling milk, try to keep him as far away as possible so that his presence does not put people off. Special overalls and gloves are advisable for the handler to wear, especially if the same person has to deal with both the male and the milk! This smell is produced chiefly from glands on the head behind the horns, and they can be partially inactivated when he is disbudded. However, during the breeding season, not only do the glands become more active, but he adds to the smell by spraying urine all over his front legs and face. To us this seems extraordinary, but the females are attracted by this scent which is certainly enhanced by this peculiar practice! The whole of his living accommodation will soon be permeated by the smell, as is any female goat to which he is allowed prolonged access while serving. This is one of the reasons why male goats are not normally run with dairy goats like a ram is with ewes. The other reason is that when you are supplying either retail or wholesale outlets with milk, the buyers demand a steady supply, so that it is vital to spread out your kiddings as much as possible. If the male was running with the herd, they would all be served during September and October, and would be dry by December or January when the demand is very high.

MATING

It is usual, in any case, for pedigree goats to be mated in-hand. This is not quite what it sounds! It simply means that the female is led to the male's house, he is brought out and they are observed mating, then parted at once. It sounds a little clinical and brief, but prolonged play will only result in a very smelly milker, and a tired-out male.

When a female is properly in season, she is very willing and will stand still wagging her tail at the male, who will mount her after perhaps only a preliminary 'woffling' sound made with the head outstretched. The act of mating is extremely brief in goats and is all over almost before you have noticed. The male will often show that it has been performed by grunting and throwing back his head, and the female will sometimes arch her back, but this is all done in a matter of seconds. When the male dismounts it is best to remove him straightaway as he is more amenable at this time. If a second service is desired, this can be performed later in the day, or the next day, but there is no point in allowing a second one straightaway unless there was some doubt about the first. Some owners of stud males prefer to put the female in the male's pen and let him serve her there, but I find this more awkward to manage, as you then have to take her away from him at some point, which makes him more cross than does leading him away from her when outside.

It may sound rather obvious, but a female goat can only be served when she is in season, or more correctly, in oestrus. Goats are naturally seasonal breeders and under normal conditions will come into season every twenty-one days from about September to February. When there is no male present, this will sometimes be delayed until October or even November. The peak of the breeding season is from about mid-November to January, and goats are very fertile at this time. Early and late in the season the signs of oestrus can be very slight and the receptive period brief, but otherwise goats are usually in season for between one and three days each time. It is not wise to rely on a third day, especially if you have to travel to a male. It is always best to mate her when she is at the peak of the season, probably within twenty-four hours of seeing the first signs. If you have your own male it will be easy for you to tell when goats are ready, as you can always test them taking them to his house. Male goats are liable to make advances to any female (or even male!) goat at this time of the year, but he will normally lose interest after a while if she is not wagging at him.

The signs to watch for in the female are restlessness, constant bleating, sometimes a slightly pink vulva which will show a clear discharge, often adhering to the tail, which she will wag frequently. Mounting behaviour, as seen in cattle, can be rather unreliable in goats unless accompanied by other signs. The goat may try to get out, or wander all around the field bleating, and in other ways behave differently from normal. In milking goats the udder often feels a little hard, and the milk may be less or more, sometimes with fidgeting behaviour apparent at milking. Of course not all goats show these signs, but most show at least two of them. If you are not sure, make a note of the date to see if she does the same things twenty-one days later. Occasionally, right at the start of the breeding season, a few goats will have a false season about five to seven days before the true ones begin. Therefore, if a goat has a vague sign in September, and you have no male of your own, it is sometimes wiser to wait and see in case she does come on more strongly in a week's time before settling into the normal three-week cycle.

TRAVELLING TO A STUD MALE

If you have to travel to a male, it is a good idea to test the goat before making the journey, with something such as a rag or collar smelling strongly of billy. An in-season goat will normally wag her tail vigorously at the scent and then you can be sure.

Having made an arrangement, probably by telephone, with the stud owner, please do your best to arrive at the agreed time as they are very busy people at that time of the year and may have other callers for the same male later.

Goats usually travel well, whether in the back of an estate car, van or trailer. If the floor is slippery, do use some straw or old matting otherwise she will have a very uncomfortable ride trying to get a grip with her feet. Many will lie down, so do not tie her collar unless absolutely necessary. In a car it is wise to use a dog-guard or homemade partition to prevent her from jumping in with the driver! The more comfortably she travels, the more chance there is of a successful mating.

The goat society stud list will enable you to choose a suitable mate with the qualities you are seeking. If you have small goats, a male kid may be best, not in the hope that he will throw smaller kids, but because the actual service is easier if the goats are fairly well matched, although males are usually bigger than females. A very large male can flatten a goatling!

If she is unwilling and will not wag her tail and stand to the male, you have brought her either too soon or too late. If you are fairly sure it is the former, the stud owner may be able to accommodate her overnight in case she comes on the next morning. If you are new to it all, please take the word of the male's owner, and his advice, as he or she will be knowledgeable in these matters and it is no use trying to force a goat if she is not properly in season. It is tempting to assume that animals have human feelings, and think that she may be afraid of the billy if it is 'her first time', but it really does not work like that. Although she may be momentarily put off by an uncomfortable journey, she really has only one thing in mind when in season, and will often drag the handler off to the male house the minute she gets a whiff of him.

The fee is paid at the time and you will then be given a

service certificate with the male's name and number on it. If the goat should come in season again in three weeks you are entitled to at least one more free service. However, goats are very fertile and normally, if you see no signs of season for the next six weeks, you can assume she is in kid.

STAGGERING THE MATINGS

When you take your newly served goat home, smelling of billy, all the rest of the herd may well come in season, so you will have to plan carefully for a continuous milk supply. The most usual arrangement is to mate all dry goatlings, goats who have run through from the previous year, and poor milkers as early as possible to kid in February or early March. Others can then be dealt with in the middle of the season, or you can leave them all to be mated late, in about January. This would apply to goats who milk well in the winter, and by kidding them in June, they will be milking well for the following winter too. Finally, you may wish to serve your previous spring's kids when they are about ten months to one year, providing that they have grown enough. This means that they should have reached about 60 per cent of their expected adult weight, and should be at least 80-90lb (35-40kg).

There are various means by which commercial goatkeepers are able to kid their goats out of season nowadays. This is a great bonus as it means that you can have a more consistent supply of milk. When goats are run through, which is the traditional way of providing winter milk, they will increase in yield again in the spring exactly at the same time as all the others are kidding. Hence there is always a flood of milk at the one time. Goats will occasionally kid naturally in autumn or winter if a male (preferably a young one, who will not be too smelly) is allowed to run with the herd from late spring to about August. This is a rather unreliable method, but assistance can be given by adjusting the lighting of the goathouse to fool the goats into thinking that it is autumn when it is not. It is chiefly the decreasing day length that triggers goats to come into season so if you can increase the light artificially from January to March and then reduce light to normal, goats can sometimes be encouraged to come in season in May. This method is particularly suited to housed herds, and the lighting will need to be efficient and modern. This system does not always work, and there are other artificial means that can be employed. By the use of impregnated vaginal sponges and a hormone injection, goats can be made to come on heat in summer. This system was made for sheep, but has been found to work as well in goats. The sponges are inserted after the longest day, removed after about a fortnight, the goat having been given the necessary injection, and she should come in season a couple of days later. She will then kid from mid-December on. The sponges and equipment have to be obtained from your vet, and you should discuss it with him or her then. Some people have a dislike of artificial means, and there are undoubtedly a few snags which can occur, such as goats having multiple births, as many as four or five at a time. The product is quite expensive, you have to have male goats ready to work out of season and in addition, it does occasionally fail to work at all. It is probably best to avoid such methods until you are familiar with your goats' normal breeding cycle and kidding.

Artificial insemination is now available for goats, and would certainly combat the problem of having a male ready out of season. It is organised by a firm called COBS, and the name and address of your nearest inseminator can be obtained from COBS or your local goat society. As the scheme is fairly new, the BGS may have to be contacted for an up-to-date list of operators. By using AI you will have access to some of the very best males in the country, different blood lines from those at stud in your area, and all without the smell!

CHAPTER SEVEN

PREGNANCY AND KIDDING

Goats are still very natural animals, in that man has not interfered too much with their original shape. Consequently, as a rule, they are blessed with very trouble-free pregnancies and kidding. Of course things can go wrong, sometimes simply through bad luck, and at other times because of incorrect management; a common fault is over-feeding during early pregnancy, causing fat to be deposited on the internal organs. This can lead to all sorts of problems such as pregnancy toxaemia or a difficult birth.

The embryos are very small during the first three months and only begin to take a great deal out of the mother in the final six weeks or so. The feeding in those early stages should be just adequate for her own body needs and the amount of milk she is giving. In the case of the non-milking first kidder, it is important to keep the concentrate feeding at a low level in the early months, but offer ample roughage. The goats' gestation is near enough five calendar months. We always work out our herd's kidding dates in this way and are rarely more than a day or two out either way. Therefore, if a goat was served on the 21st October, she will kid about the 21st March.

PREGNANCY TESTING

In the past there were no reliable pregnancy tests for goats, and it was just a matter of guess-work and hoping that they were in kid. As I have mentioned, goats are very fertile, so you can be reasonably sure that if one does not come in season again within six weeks of being served, she is pregnant. Although there are some signs that can be observed by the experienced, it is very difficult to tell just by looking at a goat whether or not she is in kid. The size of her abdomen is very deceiving and a goat who looks very pregnant is often just the one who is not.

There are now one or two pregnancy tests which can be carried out on goats. The new tests involve either ultra-sound scanning, or hormone tests done on milk or blood. For the ultra-sound test you will need the services of someone with the very expensive equipment. Some vets have it, otherwise you can contact one of the contractors whose sole job is to go around to flocks of sheep, scanning them for pregnancy. The technique is the same for goats and some of these people have become just as skilled with goats as with sheep. These ultra-sound devices either use a listening method, or a picture on a screen. Either way, the results are very accurate and it is also possible for a skilled operator to detect cloudburst, which is the name used for false pregnancy in goats. A test can also be done on the milk, and this can either be carried out by the Milk Marketing Board, or it is now possible to buy your own testing set. This would be a useful tool for the goat farmer with large numbers to test. Otherwise, in a non-milking goat, the vet can take a blood sample to be sent away for examination.

Apart from these accurate tests, an experienced goatkeeper can often tell that a goat is pregnant by noting subtle signs like a puffiness of the skin around the vulva, or the goat grunting and sighing a great deal while lying down. For some reason this is often very noticeable in Anglo Nubians. The most obvious pointer is the decline and drying up of the milk at about two months before she is due. A few goats of heavy milking strains can be difficult to dry off, and I would not advocate just leaving them unmilked if they are still giving several pints a day. If they will not dry off by the usual method of milking every other time and then every other day, you may have to milk them at least occasionally before kidding. Goats seem to have a much stronger inclination to milk than cows and serious udder trouble can arise from trying to dry them off drastically. Once the yield is reduced to less than one pint a day, she can usually be left unmilked safely for the remainder of the pregnancy.

If a goat is difficult to dry off, or has any sign of mastitis during that lactation, I would insert a 'dry cow' tube. This is obtained from your vet who will explain its use. It is a plastic syringe with a nozzle instead of a needle, filled with a long-acting antibiotic. This is inserted carefully into the teat end and the plunger depressed. This is done when the goat is virtually dry and she would not, if possible, be milked again until kidding. The aim is to leave the solution in the udder, so that it works slowly for the whole of the dry period. It is very important to comply with the manufacturer's instructions on the matter of how long to withhold milk. Any milk drawn from the udder during this dry period must not be used for human consumption. Even if you prefer not to use antibiotics at other times, these tubes do aid the healing process for any udder that has been damaged or had infection during the previous lactation. I would be rather suspicious of any goat who does not seem to be drying off at all at the normal time, and unless there are definite signs of pregnancy (not just a fat belly), it would be as well to have a test.

CARE DURING PREGNANCY

During pregnancy, especially in the first three months, all the goat needs in the way of attention is good roughage such as hay, silage or grass, a little concentrate, freedom from both internal and external parasites, and a final foot trim about two months before she is due. Exercise is desirable, but not vital if difficult to provide. It is a fact that many goats are heavily in kid just at the worst time of the year as far as weather is concerned, and out-door exercise is not always possible. Routine vaccination should be carried out before kidding, which will give the kids their first protection (see Chapter 9).

It is always worth remembering that pregnancy and parturition are natural events and not illnesses. The human being has endowed the whole process with an air of drama, science and interference, which animals mercifully do not usually need or want. The great majority of animals give birth with no difficulty whatsoever, par-ticularly if kept in or near their natural state. Although we have domesticated the goat, I would class her along with the mongrel bitch and the farm cat, in the matter of trouble-free birth. It is usual for goats to kid unaided, but it is wise to observe from a tactful distance in case of problems. It would be foolish to disregard the possibility of trouble altogether, so you should be vigilant. A closed circuit television system, such as that used by some thoroughbred horse breeders would be very handy, although I have never found goats to be disturbed by quiet human observation.

Often goats are settled down for the night with absolutely no sign of imminent kidding, only for the owner to find the kids, clean and licked, running about the pen in the morning. On the other hand, the careful breeder will attempt to be on hand for as many kiddings as possible, but do not feel guilty if you miss some; they were likely to have been the quickest and easiest anyway.

PREPARATION FOR KIDDING

The arrangements that you make for kidding will depend on your method of housing. Some people with large groups of loose-housed goats allow them to kid where they are, finding that the other goats move away. However there are advantages in the kidding taking place in an individual pen, especially if any assistance is needed. Also, some goats will 'steal' other goats' kids thus depriving them of the vital colostrum from their own dam. Even if you normally keep your goats in separate pens, you may prefer, as we do, to use special spare pens kept aside for the purpose. The pens should be as large as possible, have solid kid-proof walls, especially at floor level, preferably no water bucket for the kid to fall into, plenty of clean bedding and good natural and artificial lighting. Incidently, there is no reason at all why a goat should not kid out of doors in the field, providing that the weather is mild. It is clean and healthy out in the fresh air, and she will usually seek a sheltered corner away from the herd. You should still prepare a pen in which to bring her and the young family to later.

Goats can be a week early or a week late, but kidding outside these times is quite rare. Early kidding often indicates triplets or even more, and single kids are often a few days late. This is not a hard and fast rule though!

The first noticeable signs that a goat is a few days away from kidding are the enlargement and filling of the udder, the kids dropping down lower into the belly, and hollows appearing either side of the tail. If the udder becomes very tight, several days early, and there are no other signs that she is about to kid, it may be necessary to milk her a little to ease the udder. The sticky yellow colostrum milk should be retained for the kid and can be frozen.

The hollows at either side of the tail become more noticeable as kidding nears, with the final part of the spine, where it joins the tail, standing up like a ridge. The skin around the vulva looks very soft and puffy, and the udder usually appears much shinier on the final day. Eventually you will begin to notice odd behaviour in the goat. She may eat large amounts of hay ravenously, and may be standing up more than usual with sometimes a gazing, faraway look in her eyes. She will certainly become restless, and talk gently to you every time you approach. In the morning she may not want to go out with the others, or fail to come in with them at milking time. Pawing at the bedding, getting up and lying down frequently, are signs often seen. Quite often though, goats appear to be unmoved by the first stage of labour, and only show that something is happening when the actual expulsion of the kid is about to start.

Once she has got to this stage, a thick white fluid will appear at the vulva. Before this you may have observed a clearer, thinner discharge. Now you can be sure that kidding is really under way, although the kid may not appear for a while after straining really begins. A kid should have been produced within about half an hour of the thick discharge being seen. Many goats lie down to strain, although not all, and soon you will see a balloon-like bag which serves to open and lubricate the passage. This will often burst and is followed by the kid enclosed in another bag. Hopefully, the kid will be in the correct position, rather like a diver, with the two front feet one behind the other, closely followed by the nose. At this stage, the goat will often cry out, and if you want to assist, you should pull gently downwards on the feet as the head is born. This may take a while if the kid is big, so do not be impatient, although it is natural to want to help the goat get it over with. Once the head is out, the rest of the kid quickly follows. It will fall to the ground and the cord will break naturally especially if the goat kidded while standing. The goat will usually start to lick the kid straightaway, but if she is unwilling, encourage her by putting it near her head, and wipe its nose clear of slime if she fails to do so. Kids often get onto their feet very quickly and start searching for milk at once.

The second kid is usually born quickly after the first, but there can be a delay of perhaps half an hour. Goats can have five or even six kids, but up to three is more usual. The more she has, the more help she may need in attending to them, and cleaning them. Quads and quins are likely to be small, and may need assistance to begin breathing. If a goat has a male kid that is going to be destroyed, you can take it away at birth, providing that the mother has at least one kid left to fuss over. Otherwise you can take unwanted kids away later, at the same time as you remove the females to the kids' house. Remember that the goat does not know that one is going to be kept and the other destroyed or reared for meat. The responsibility is yours, and you must make the parting of the kids and mother as humane as possible for her sake (see page 81).

DEALING WITH THE NEWBORN KID

You will probably be anxious to see what sex the kids are, and unlike rabbits for example, sex is very easy to determine at birth. Amazingly, some people do find it difficult and are confused by the small teats present in all kids, male and female. All male mammals have rudimentary teats if you think about it! Female kids look just like a miniature version of the mother, and male kids have a noticeable furry bag between the hind legs, the scrotum. This can be easily determined by touch in a bad light.

Once the kids are up on their feet, they will be searching for the teats, and having found them will begin sucking. If they cannot seem to find the right place, or have difficulty in getting the end of the teat in their mouths, then you should assist them. Kids are not easy to guide to the teat, greatly resenting having their heads pushed. If the goat has long hanging teats, and the kids are looking for them too high up, then you can lift up the teat towards the kid. This is often more successful than trying to push the kid in the right direction. I find that it is often better to feed an awkward but hungry kid from a bottle than to attempt to place it onto the teat. If your kids are going to be hand-reared anyway, then feeding will be easier if they have had their first feed from a bottle. It is vital that they should have had a feed of colostrum within six hours of birth, as the essential antibodies it contains are best absorbed by the kid at that time. If the mother dies, has no milk, or is otherwise ill, the colostrum from another freshly kidded goat, preferably from the same herd, is the best substitute. For this reason it is always wise to keep a supply of frozen colostrum for emergencies, which is easily done, as most goats give far more than is needed by their own kids.

CARE OF THE DAM AFTER KIDDING

After kidding most goats appreciate a long drink of tepid water, after which, clean straw should be shaken over the soiled bedding. The kids' navels should be dressed with either iodine, antiseptic powder, or antibiotic spray, then there is nothing further to be done, and the family should be left in peace. I know this is difficult, especially if they are your first kids!

You will still have to look in once or twice to check that the afterbirth has been expelled. After the final kid is born, a thin string can be seen hanging from the goat, which indicates that the placenta is still inside. The time gap after the birth of the last kid and the afterbirth expulsion can be brief, or a matter of several hours. There is actually one afterbirth for each kid, but they often come out together, and it is not a pleasant job, sorting through to determine how many pieces there are. However, if nothing is left hanging from the goat, you can be fairly sure that it has all passed out. Many goats eat the placenta, which is perfectly natural, and does not seem to be harmful, but many authorities say that it is better taken away for burial. I have never seen a goat come to any harm from eating them, but do usually take them out of the pen for disposal if I can.

If the placenta does not come away, it is imperative that you do not attempt to pull it out yourself. It may tear and leave portions behind, or you may bring on serious bleeding. If it has not come out within twelve hours of the birth, telephone the vet to ask his advice. He may suggest leaving it for another few hours, after which he will come and remove it himself, or, as is more usual now, prescribe antibiotic injections daily, until it has come out. This usually only takes a couple more days, but if the goat is left without this antibiotic cover, she could develop a serious womb infection, from which she may not recover. I would always use all these modern aids to healing in a case like this, as antibiotics have prevented the suffering and death of many goats with metritis (see page 118).

After a goat has kidded, she will have a bloody discharge, which often becomes heavier about a week after kidding and may continue, gradually decreasing, for about three weeks. If it continues too long, or is very offensive, speak to the vet about it. It is not easy to keep the tail clean during this time and many goats object strongly to having it washed. In a large herd, this daily washing would be impractical, and it will therefore be necessary to wait until the goat has stopped bleeding before removing the soiled hair from the tail.

ASSISTED KIDDINGS

Having covered the events that take place during a normal kidding, I must now mention a few things that can go wrong, although I must stress that these are comparatively rare.

Probably the most common difficulty arises when the kid or kids are in the wrong position. I do not propose to describe in great detail how to sort out misplaced kids, as I think that this is a job for the experienced goatkeeper, shepherd, or vet. Sometimes it is simply a matter of common sense and a little adjustment. It goes without saying, that before any manipulation is performed, your hands must be washed thoroughly and lubricated with soap lather, or obstetrical jelly. One position seen frequently is that of the head and only one foot coming out. It is often possible to find the other foot close behind and pull it forward, but otherwise it is possible to deliver the kid as it is. A goat often succeeds in bringing forth a kid in this position unaided, and indeed it is sometimes easier for her when it is a large kid, than the correct position. If the two front feet are presented with no head, investigate gently, and if the head is turned back, the kid will have to be pushed right back into the goat before any attempt can be made to bring the head round. If the head only is out, and investigation fails to find the legs close behind, attempt to push the head back in, with ample lubrication. If the goat was unattended for some time, before being found with the kid's head in this position, the natural lubrication may have drained away, making it very difficult to get the head back in. This sort of procedure certainly needs a skilled person, and if in any doubt call the vet.

Another very common position is that of the breech birth. The second of twins is often born hind feet first, and this is quite normal. There is nothing to concern you unless the birth is slow, in which case it is wise to help the kid out, as it can die or suffer brain damage if the cord is pinched while the head is still in the mother. After delivering one of these, it is a good idea to hang it upside down for a while to let any fluid drain out. If only a tail is showing, you should really push it back in and feel for the legs, but in practice, a small kid, especially if not the first born, will often slip out easily as he is.

Occasionally, two kids will try to come out at once, in which case, you will see that there is the wrong number of legs presented, or one hind and one fore. If this is the case, attempt to feel which kid is coming first, and push the other one back. This can sometimes be done easily, but again, if in doubt, call for help. If a goat has been straining and pushing for perhaps half an hour, and nothing is showing, investigate with a lubricated hand, and if you can find nothing, call the vet. There could be a dead kid curled into a ball, a very large kid in the wrong position, or the neck of the womb may have failed to dilate properly.

It really is important to call for help at an early stage, if, having investigated, you cannot sort it out easily yourself. Never mess about with a goat until she is exhausted, dry and sore, before getting assistance. Vets much prefer being called out on a false alarm, only to find that the goat has kidded, than having to deal with a damaged and suffering animal.

It is usual, after any assisted kidding, for the goat to have an antibiotic injection to avoid the risk of infection. Metritis can carry a goat off very swiftly, and is best avoided by this precaution. If she seems at all off-colour a day or so after kidding, consult the vet without delay.

REMOVING THE KIDS

Assuming that you are going to be taking the kids away for hand-rearing at some point, you will have to decide when to affect the separation. In my view, this can be done without great distress to either the mother or kid, if done carefully.

One of the reasons why we kid our goats in a different pen from the one they normally live in, is that after the kid is taken to the kid house, the mother soon settles down on returning to her own pen. The familiar smell of her pen, her companions beside her, and most important, no scent or sound of the kid to remind her, are all helpful to her peace of mind.

We feel it is important to remove the kid from its mother much earlier than the four days suggested by many goat books. Presumably the reason for choosing four days is because this is the usual length of time before selling the milk. During those days it becomes progressively more like milk and less like colostrum. As I have said, it is essential that the kid receives sufficient colostrum, and it is best if the first vital few feeds are taken in the dam's presence; for the remaining time it is immaterial if the milk is given via a bottle or the udder. We have found that if the separation is carried out at about twenty-four hours after birth, the upset to both parties is far less than if a stronger bond is allowed to develop. In addition, the kids take to the artificial teat much more readily at that time before they have become too imprinted on the udder. I feel that the whole process is kind and humane when done in this way.

If it is the time of the year when the goats are going out to graze, the mother goat is let out with the herd and the kids only removed when she is out of the way. If the herd is fully housed at the time, then the kids are taken while the mother is occupied being milked, before being returned to her own pen. Taking the kids away without her seeing is important, and you will find that goats fuss and call very little when it is done in this way, except while waiting for milking time. This is because the goat tends to transfer her affections to the person who milks, and calls to him or her every time she sees him during the first few days.

MALE KIDS AND UNWANTED FEMALES

Many of the kids will of course be taken to the kid house for rearing (see Chapter 8), but it may well be that some are going to have to be destroyed. The decision whether to put some kids down at birth is a very tricky one, which should be made before the kids are born if possible. In the past, goatkeepers have always been advised that, unless a kid is good enough for breeding, implying almost all males and a few females as well, they should be put down at birth. Now, however, increasing numbers of people, both domestic goatkeepers and farmers, are rearing some for meat. A kid reared to about four months old produces an excellent lean carcass of delicious meat. The economics for the private goatkeeper, who may otherwise be buying meat from the butcher, are very favourable, especially if surplus milk would otherwise go to waste. As far as the commercial goatkeeper is concerned, the rewards are not so great; all the milk would otherwise be sold, and labour has to be costed. In spite of the difficulties, quite a few are developing good outlets for this meat as a by-product of the dairy herd, and it is certainly a reasonable alternative to the unpleasant task of despatching newborn animals.

If you have decided not to rear male kids for meat, then I can only repeat the advice given by all the goat societies; that it is far better to put them down than to give them away as pets. I feel that the commercial goatkeeper is less likely to be tempted to 'find them good homes' than the smaller more sentimental goatkeeper, but it still needs to be said. Male kids, with very few exceptions, do not make good pets, and are almost invariably abandoned, passed on, or otherwise disposed of, at some later date, often having spent a miserable existence with insufficient food and attention.

The same thing applies to female kids with serious faults, or those from very poor milkers. Female kids who are surplus to the herd simply on account of there being too many, may well be found suitable buyers as future domestic goats, but the breeder should always be prepared to send them for meat if they do not sell. It is rarely possible to obtain a good enough price for goatlings to justify keeping them until they are in kid, and no smallholder or farmer can afford to sell them for a lower price than the rearing costs. Youngstock from milk recorded herds will usually sell well, and may be suitable for export if well bred. All this sounds callous, but it is advice frequently repeated by such respected bodies as the British Goat Society, and is not merely a financial attitude.

Before deciding which female kids to keep they should be inspected carefully to determine that everything is normal with their teats, sexual organs, jaws, etc. Some faults are more serious than others, and few farmers would put down a good kid for mismarked colour or misplaced tassels. However, serious teat abnormalities like double or two-holed teats, or a very under- or over-shot jaw, means that the kid should never be bred from. Anglo Nubians often have a slightly short top jaw, and if this is really only to a slight degree, it is not always considered a serious fault. Likewise, many farmers used to cows would not cull a kid for a small supernumary teat when it is blind and well away from the proper ones. It should be born in mind though, that this sort of abnormality is hereditary and the mating that produced it should not be repeated.

Kids should also be examined to be sure that they are not 'hermaphrodites' or inter-sex. These are not true hermaphrodites, as that would imply that they are both male and female. In fact these kids are neither male nor female, but somewhere in between, and obviously are not capable of breeding. Many look like almost normal females until later in life, when at puberty they become aggressive and masculine. They are nearly always polled, being also the product of two polled parents. This is by no means always the case, and they do occasionally occur from horned goats. Although you are always taking this risk when mating two polled goats together, it is only rarely that it results in hermaphrodites, but this makes it difficult to breed a pure polled line of goats. A typical hermaphrodite will have the outer female sex organs further away from the anus than usual, and they are likely to be enlarged. If in doubt, show the kid to an experienced goatkeeper or vet.

Having, hopefully, only a small number of kids to put down each year, you will have to decide how to go about it. I do not want to gloss over this unpleasant subject, but it causes a great deal of worry to some people. There are a number of readers who would be able to do the job themselves, some of them farmers used to despatching rabbits, hens and perhaps deformed piglets or lambs. Obviously, if you have a humane killer, or a suitable gun, there is no problem as long as you know how to use it. Others may still be able to get chloroform, which used to be freely available from the chemist, and was in my opinion, one of the more humane methods. Alternatively, your vet may be prepared to let you have something. If none of these aids is available, and you are skilled at killing rabbits by means of a sharp blow to the back of the neck, it is possible to kill newborn kids in the same way. I stress that the person doing it *must* know what he is doing and be satisfied that it will be instantaneous. Other methods, such as drowning, are much frowned upon as being far too slow, and should not be considered.

There are many people who will not have either the wherewithal, or the willpower, to do any of the above, and must have another person to put their kids down. The vet is an obvious choice, but is rather expensive for a goat farm which may have a large number of kids. Most hunt kennels will shoot them for you for no charge, but you would have to take the kids there. Likewise a knacker would do it, but would be unlikely to want to travel for such small animals. I would not suggest trying such societies as the RSPCA, because, unless the kid is sick, they may try to persuade you to let them find it a 'home'.

CARE OF THE LACTATING GOAT

Having dealt with that unpleasant but necessary subject, we will now return to the freshly kidded goat. Normally, she will need little special care as she starts her lactation, but there are a few details to keep an eye on. When the kids are on her for the first day or so, they may only feed from one side of the udder, even when there are three kids. In this case it is important to take a little milk from the other side, to even up the udder. If this is not done, and the udder left unattended for a few days, she may either develop mastitis, or the yield will begin to dry up on that side. In any case, she would become very uncomfortable, and the more tender that half becomes, the less likely she is to allow the kids to suck, thereby setting up a vicious circle.

Do not milk her right out until the fourth day, unless she is giving very little, because by encouraging too rapid an increase in milk production, you could set off milk-fever (see page 117). Freshly kidded goats drink a great deal of water, and the intake will increase as the yield builds up. In very cold weather it is wise to give warm water to these goats, at least temporarily. Some books suggest feeding bran mashes, for example, instead of the normal concentrates for the first few days, but we prefer to give our goats just a small amount of the usual feed, only gradually building up to the proper production ration.

A milking goat will lose some weight during the first three months of lactation, and it is important to keep her eating well to avoid metabolic disturbances such as acetoneamia. High energy foods such as flaked maize and sugar beet are good preventatives, and some people find cider vinegar added to the feed, beneficial. It can certainly do no harm and does seem to aid digestion. It is also important to lessen the worm burden at this time, and to this end, we always dose ours just before or just after kidding, unless they have not been out since the previous worming. This is quite safe if you use products such as Panacur or Multispec for worming.

Providing that they are now fed as recommended in Chapter 4, your lactating goats will now become established milkers, and should continue to milk well for one or even two years.

CHAPTER EIGHT

KID REARING

It is always tempting to keep more youngstock than you really should, especially when you are improving and enlarging your herd, perhaps grading up to pedigree status. It is important to be firm with yourself, and bear in mind that the profits from the milking herd will be depleted if you rear too many kids. It costs a great deal to rear a batch of kids well, and this cost will be a drain on any profit you make. Decide on the number of kids you wish to rear as replacements, keep only those from your very best milkers, and stick to your decision. For a herd of about fifty milkers, between six and nine kids a year for replacement should be ample.

There are various methods of rearing kids, and while the more modern systems are likely to appeal to the goat farmer, I must mention briefly the more traditional ones. The way that a kid is reared can affect her whole life, future milk production, and health, the first six months being undoubtedly the most important time. It is no use having a top-quality pedigree kid and ruining her by bad rearing, and conversely, there is little point in acquiring a free or cheap kid of unknown breeding, only to find that after rearing her well, she does not have the genetic make-up to yield heavily.

NATURAL REARING

It is, of course, possible to leave the kids on the dam and let her rear them the natural way. You may think that this must be the best way, and although it is the norm for Angora, feral and other non-dairy goats, it has great disadvantages in a milking herd. When reared on the mother, the kid obtains plenty of milk at the right temperature, needs very little human attention, and will usually grow well, learning to graze at an early age. However, the snags of natural rearing for the commercial dairy herd are many and varied. As far as the kid is concerned, she will not be tame, and as a result nothing like as easy to handle and to milk when the times comes, as a hand-reared kid. She cannot be sold until fully weaned and her wildness puts off potential buyers. Furthermore, when youngsters are running with adult goats, there are parasite and other disease risks.

The disadvantages for your milk supply are even greater. The goat will almost certainly yield less milk than one fully hand or machine milked, and will often be unco-operative as she is trying to hold back milk for the kid. If you wish to officially record your herd, or even simply keep your own private records, there is no way that you can tell what the goat's true yield is. So, while there are some advantages of natural rearing for the owner of house goats, there really are none for dairy herds.

ARTIFICIAL REARING

When our kids are first taken away form their mothers, we put them into small pens, usually made from four pallets joined at the corners. Kids must be bedded deeply, with thick straw, and if the floor is concrete you can keep out the chill by putting down old paper feed sacks or cardboard underneath the straw. This should only be done for young kids, as the older ones will paw up the bedding and tear the paper! We put several kids, usually up to four, to a pen to keep each other warm. All draughts should be excluded from this small pen, and if the weather is very cold, a partial lid or roof can be placed over the back of the pen. We only use a heat lamp in very extreme conditions, or if only a single kid is available to occupy a pen. If your kid accommodation consists of large roomy pens or loose boxes, then a wooden box placed on its side will serve as a 'nest' for the kids to sleep in.

There are now various devices for feeding lambs and kids; lamb-bars, buckets with teats attached, and even automatic warm milk machines. The scale of your operations, the cost of the equipment, and the number of kids to be reared, will determine what method you choose. Without a doubt, the cheapest and simplest method is the bottle and teat, and it is also the easiest one to teach to the kid. It is surprisingly simple and quick to feed them on bottles as long as they are in the type of pens that enable you to push the teat through the bars without the kids having to come out and mill about your legs. This is the method we prefer, having tried

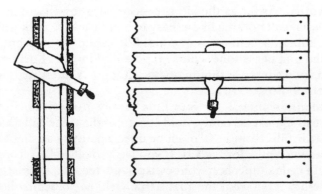

A simple way to hold bottles for kid feeding

other means, and can rear up to thirty kids spread over the season, providing that they are in pens of four kids each. A pallet used as the front of the pen, makes it easy to push a row of bottles through to rest on one of the bars. By this means we can feed two pens of kids at the same time, as once the bottles are in place, they need little support (see illustration).

There are a number of different teats available and everybody has his own favourite. These teats are not made specifically for kids, and if you have reared lambs on the bottle you will recognise them as lamb teats. There are two particularly suitable types, the simplest and cheapest being the black and red plug-in type which will fit most wine or spirit bottles. This is made either with or without an air vent, and we much prefer the former, because without a vent, the kid is sucking against a vacuum all the time, and takes much longer to feed. The hole provided in teats is always too small and we enlarge it with a small cross in the end made with a sharp knife. Incidently, these teats will drip milk from the vent during feeding while the kids are still small, but once they begin to suck hard in a week or so, the dripping stops as the vent begins to work as it should. Plug-in teats must fit the bottles tightly.

There is a newer type of teat, also having an air vent, but a valve as well, to prevent any dripping. This screws onto the bottle, making it impossible for the kid to pull it off, but it can be difficult to find bottles with the right screw to fit. The pint-size cheese rennet bottles are very good for small kids, and a plastic pop bottle is suitable for feeding larger amounts. These teats are smaller and softer than the plug-in ones, and therefore, easier for baby kids to start on. It is quite a simple matter to teach a kid of only a day or two old to feed from a rubber teat, but a more difficult task if the kid has been left on the dam longer. In that case the kid will have to be left until really hungry before she will tolerate the artificial teat.

It can be more difficult to teach kids to use the lamb-bar type teats, which are normally attached to the front of the pen and have tubes running from the teats down into containers of milk. There is another feeder made like a large lidded bucket with teats all around the base. Gravity, in this type, makes it easier for the kids to suck out the milk, but it is rather expensive. Variations made on the same principle are now available, some in the form of a long trough with teats attached, which hang over the pen partition.

Apart from deciding on which feeding device to use, there is a choice between warm, restricted milk feeding, cold milk ad lib, or warm ad lib. For the latter you would need one of the very expensive machines. We use warm milk fed three times daily, and as I have said, we do like bottle feeding, especially for female kids, as it tends to make them very human-orientated and tame. You can be sure that each kid is getting her full ration and any necessary medicine can be given in the bottle. If female kids are being reared for sale, any purchaser can easily continue with bottle feeding without having to buy any special equipment, other than the teat.

Milk Powder
The question of which milk or milk substitute to use causes a great deal of discussion among goatkeepers. Of course, goats' milk is the best, but it is rare for a commercial goatkeeper to have sufficient to spare from his sales, and the value of this milk when sold makes it very expensive for kid rearing. There appears to be very little difference between kids reared on the different makes and types of powder, providing upsets like scouring are kept at bay. They can safely be given one of these milk substitutes after the first few days when the colostrum has all been used up. There are now several milk powders on the market made especially for kids and these are excellent, if a little expensive. Unlike calf milks,

they have no antibiotic growth-promoters added. All milk powders for animal feeding, whether designed for kids, calves, lambs, foals, or even babies, are based on dried cows' milk, with modifications to make them a substitute for the real mothers' milk. Nowadays these all seem to be of good quality. While you may wish to use a purpose-made kid substitute for rearing good female kids, it is not economical to use these for meat kids, because all costs have to be kept to a minimum to make it worth doing at all. Ordinary calf powder can be used, or the cheaper whey-based ones, which we have found to be very satisfactory, both for males and females, and have not had any problems with their use. At the time of writing, the cost of a 25 kg bag is much lower than most kid milk. Providing that the milk substitute is introduced slowly by increasing the amount fed only a little at a time, the kids take to it without scouring. Lamb milk powder is not as good, being very expensive and unnecessarily rich for kids.

Quantity to feed
When using bottles or lamb-bar warm milk feeding, kids are usually fed three times a day to begin with, the quantity of milk per feed beginning at between $1/4$ and $1/2$ pt (150 and 300 ml), gradually working up to about 1 pt (600 ml) or a little more as soon as the kid can take it comfortably, probably at about two to three weeks. However, as with all artificially reared animals, you must use your own judgement in respect of how much to feed. To begin with, the kids should always be left looking for more after feeding, then you can be sure that you have not overfed them. Cold ad lib systems work on the principle of having milk always before them; they ration themselves.

You may have been led to believe that kids need feeding at least four times daily, and with larger quantities than I have mentioned. It used to be recommended that they have at least 4 pt (2.3L) of milk a day and were given this for at least six months, with one bottle continuing right through the winter. Now that people are keeping goats commercially, it has been realised that this is quite unnecessary, and it is now usual to rear kids in a more up-to-date manner. There is no doubt that kids can be well-reared by either method, providing that the management is good, and today's kids do just as well as the traditionally reared ones.

Once our kids are drinking up to 3 pt (1.7L) a day, we continue to feed that amount until they are eating their concentrates well, usually at about six weeks. The middle feed is then withdrawn, and they continue with 2 pt (1.1L) daily for about another three weeks, with one bottle per day after that until weaning at about three months. Other modern goatkeepers wean earlier, but we find that this twelve week weaning suits our herd. If you wish to keep kids on milk for longer, there is no reason why you should not, but don't feel that you have to. It is, however, absolutely essential that the kids are used to eating a very good-quality concentrate feed before they are weaned. Calf or lamb nuts can be used, or a suitable goat feed. Coarse feeds are too often selectively eaten, in that some kids do not eat all of the ingredients. The mixture or pellet should contain at least 16—18 per cent protein, fed more or less ad lib in the early stages, and fed at a rate of about $1^1/_2$ lb (0.7 kg) per day per kid at weaning. At this stage it would usually be given in at least three feeds. Dry, fibrous silage, hay or straw is eaten almost from birth and water should be provided, at least no later than the time at which they stop their middle bottle. Before this age we find that they drink water very reluctantly, and it must always be given in such a way as to prevent its being fouled. Although concentrates are on offer earlier, we find that ours rarely tuck in properly until they are about four weeks old.

ILLNESS IN THE YOUNG KID

When rearing large numbers of kids in the same building, year after year, it is important that all hygienic precautions are taken to prevent the spread of disease. Like calves and lambs, kids are susceptible to various types of scouring, and if you are not vigilant, illness can spread rapidly. If the kids are all running together, especially if on an automatic feeder, they must be watched carefully, so that any sick kid can be treated promptly. Bottle-fed kids are easier in this respect, as one kid only can have a dose of medicine in the bottle, thus ensuring that it has had the correct dose. If medicine has to be added to the water or feed, you cannot always be sure that the very kid who needs it has eaten or drunk his ration.

The most usual cause of scour affecting young kids, often only five to ten days old, is *E.coli*. This normally results in bright yellow

91

diarrhoea, later turning to a watery pale yellow, which can affect the kid very suddenly and may even result in death before you can treat it. Do not confuse this with the normal bright yellow, mustard-like stool that colostrum-fed kids have for the first few days. A true scour is much less sticky and usually very profuse. We have found it most unwise to assume that a scour in that age of kid is 'just digestive', and always treat it straightaway. If any kid looks hunched up and refuses a bottle or is reluctant to feed, he or she has an antibiotic pill added to the next bottle of the day. If that is refused, then we dose the kid with a pill dissolved in a little warm water, by means of a plastic syringe in the side of the mouth. We have found this most successful with this type of scour. With very young kids you have no time to waste as they deteriorate very quickly. At the same time you can put the kid onto a calf scour replacement solution for a few feeds instead of milk, or simply give them a much reduced, diluted feed of goat's milk. Like many people, I do not like using antibiotics unnecessarily, but by giving this treatment early on, it is possible to nip the trouble in the bud, get the kids back to normal quickly, and prevent the outbreak from spreading through all the kids. You will have to discuss this with your vet in any case, in order to get the pills, which, incidently, are ones used for lambs with the same trouble. If the treatment does not work, then the vet will need to see them to determine what bug is causing the scour.

If buying in kids, never mix them with your own straightaway, as they will be carrying different bacteria, and will have no resistance to the ones you have on your farm. It is also unwise to mix kids of widely differing ages until the youngest are at least three or four months old.

When dealing with young, intensively kept animals, all hygienic precautions such as cleanliness of the teats, bottles etc, avoiding walking from older kids' bedding onto that of younger ones, are well worth taking. One of the most important health measures is to keep the pens well littered and as dry as possible. Really deep straw, topped up daily is the only answer, and we find that it pays to let this bedding become very deep before cleaning out, as the top layers seem to remain drier that way. When a batch of kids has moved on to a larger pen, the old one should be cleaned out thoroughly and left empty for some time. Steam cleaning is the only perfect means of cleansing, but washing with hot water and disinfectant is the next best thing. Our pallet kid pens are easily dismantled and taken out into the fresh air and sun when not in use. This could also be done if you are using calf pens or sheep hurdles for kid pens. Another important measure to help prevent the spread of disease is to make sure that the kids are unable to tread in their food or water containers. This is best arranged by the kids having to put their heads out of the pen in order to eat from containers in front of them. This means that not only can you see exactly how much they are eating, but you can also avoid wastage, spillage and soiling.

Coccidiosis and its control
One ailment, common, but to be avoided, in housed kids is coccidiosis. This is a parasite which lives and breeds in the intestines and results in scouring in young kids. Goats and sheep are both affected by several different coccidia, none of which can transfer from any other than these two species. It used to be thought that goats could contract rabbit or poultry coccidiosis, but this is now known not to be so. The kids almost certainly pick it up from their mothers in the first place. Adults carry it, but rarely show any ill effects, which is just as well because all goats probably have it to some degree!

If the kids are kept really well bedded and not overcrowded, it is possible that the disease will not manifest itself if the kids only ingest a small number of the parasite. However, the more kids you have, the more likely you are to have a breakdown in resistance. Far more kids are slightly affected than was ever realised, and it seems to be most common in damp parts of the country during winter and spring, when the atmosphere remains moist all day. It can also occur in outdoor kids.

Because there are different forms of the parasite, the symptoms are not always the same, but the first sign is nearly always a dark scour in kids four weeks and upwards. Unlike most other forms of scour, the kids are usually as eager for their bottles, but a failure in growth rate, and general loss of condition will be noticed. Some kids have few symptoms other than a disappointing growth rate, and a rough fluffy look about the coat. The vet can test a dung sample before giving treatment. Several different drugs can be used, some appearing to work much better than others, and the easiest way to administer these is to add them to the milk. Older kids can have it in their concentrate food, if their intake is high enough (see also Chapter 9).

THE OLDER KID

So far, I have not mentioned putting kids outdoors and this is because, for larger herds in particular, it is normal for dairy goatkeepers to rear their kids inside. This is done for several reasons, not least of which is the difficulty of getting large numbers of kids in and out every day, and back into the right pens! Another sound reason is that if the adult goats are using the land a great deal it will be contaminated with a high worm population which kids do better to avoid. If they are indoors all the time, they do not need worming unless being fed green food from areas where adult goats or sheep have grazed. Kids do not *need* green food while growing, but if you wish you can either grow crops specially, or cut weeds from your garden and orchard. If the kids are destined to be fed a variety of green foods when older, it is worth getting them accustomed to eating them. We usually start introducing these foods once they are weaned. The nutrition needed for optimum growth is provided by their milk and concentrates, with hay or silage for the important roughage necessary for rumen development.

As the kids grow, they are moved into larger pens, and it is a help if you can provide them with a concrete pen outside to play in. Otherwise, give them as much space to run about as you can, with an area of floor free from bedding if possible to keep their feet healthy. Our kids spend their first winter all together in a large pen with communal hay rack and trough, until the early spring, when they move into the milkers' house preparatory to going out with the herd. Once kids have reached the age of about six months, the protein in their feed can be reduced a little by the addition of cereal. At the same time they begin to eat a great deal more silage, which is necessary for the development of their capacity for eating and utilising grass later on. Kids become relatively trouble-free at this age, and it is tempting to overlook jobs that still have to be done, like foot trimming and de-lousing.

If a kid was born quite early in the year, it is possible to mate her in the first breeding season, *providing* she is big enough. Although mating kids used to be frowned upon by the goat fraternity, it is becoming more commonly done, even occasionally in show herds. This is because, with better animal feeds, better wormers, and goats generally growing faster, it has been realised that this early mating is often to the benefit of the goat herself. It is also of great interest to commercial goat owners, as a way of having productive goats as soon as possible. I must stress though, that the kid should be well-grown, and preferably at least nine months before mating. In my experience these young goats do not have any trouble in kidding, in fact, rather less than older goats. They do need to have a high standard of care afterwards as they are very prone to worm infestation which must be dealt with rigorously. For this reason early mating is especially suited to housed herds, where they will not have to meet this challenge. They do seem a little more inclined to suffer from ketosis after kidding (see page 115), but providing that this can be avoided, they will continue to grow while milking and will put on a great spurt of growth the following spring while running through. Although they do have a slight setback in growth at the beginning of their lactation, they do not remain stunted for life, as is sometimes claimed, and some of my biggest goats were the ones who kidded as goatlings.

If a kid is not big enough to mate at this time, she must not be overfed during her goatling year, and if on good grazing, may not need much in the way of concentrates during the best part of the summer.

DISBUDDING AND CASTRATION

Before leaving the matter of kids, the question of disbudding and castration must be dealt with. Kids are either born polled, that is naturally hornless, or with buds, which would develop into horns unless removed. There is absolutely nothing to be said in favour of horns on domestic milking goats, but they are often seen on free-running goats kept for meat or fibre, like Angoras. In practice, most people leave them on kids being reared for meat, because they are always housed in their own group, and are only kept for a few months before slaughter. At this young age, kids rarely do damage or become aggressive.

Kids should be examined for buds in the first few days of life, as, unlike calves, they should always be disbudded before about a week old. The ideal time is between three and five days, although Anglo Nubians are often slow in developing their buds and may be left a little later. Entire males being kept for stud purposes need to be disbudded as soon as possible, as their horn buds are visible at birth and grow very rapidly. If they are not to grow unsightly and dangerous, they should be removed by an experienced vet when the kid is no more than two or three days old. I emphasise 'vet' because in spite of what you may have read in earlier goat books, it is now illegal for anyone other than a vet to disbud kids, and an anaesthetic must be used. It does not matter how experienced a person is in disbudding calves, the procedure is not the same, and local anaesthetic is not suitable. Most vets use gas anaesthesia and this is certainly the best method, as the kid comes round very quickly afterwards and does not remain drugged for a considerable time, as is sometimes seen with other anaesthetics. A number of vets are now used to disbudding kids and if you want to be sure of finding one familiar with the job, ask around among other goat owners in your area. When carried out skilfully, there is no suffering, no after-effects, and none of our goats has shown any adverse symptoms even after about ten years of our vet doing up to twenty or thirty a year. Occasionally disbudding is not complete, especially in the case of males, and small pieces of horn regrow. If this happens while the kid is still young, the vet may wish to re-do it. Otherwise kids usually knock off these small loose pieces while playing.

Male kids being kept for meat do not have to be castrated if they are to be slaughtered before about four months. In this case they would be reared separately from females and after this age can begin to develop the male smell which could taint the meat. As soon as they become sexually aware, which can be as young as four and a half months, they rarely eat as well, and may not grow properly. If they are to be kept on longer than this age, or when you are new to kid rearing, it is safer to castrate them. The kindest method is by means of the rubber ring 'elastrator' device, as used for lambs. If done at the correct age of under one week, kids seem to suffer very little discomfort and are not set back at all. After this age the job has to be done by a vet, but it would be more upsetting for the kid.

A commercial herd showing a good mixture of different breeds

A British Toggenburg male goat, showing how a large tyre can be used for effective tethering

A crossbred 'British' goatling

Goats are usually eager to come in at milking time

The shape of udder best suited to machine milking

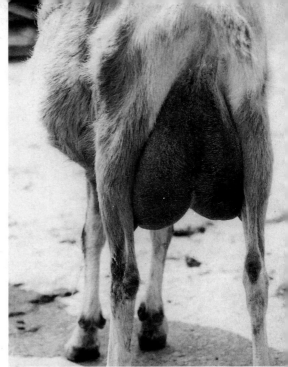

Fullwood & Bland milking machine in use

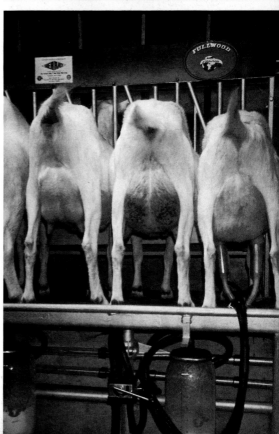

A small bucket unit for milking goats

The bucket unit milker in use

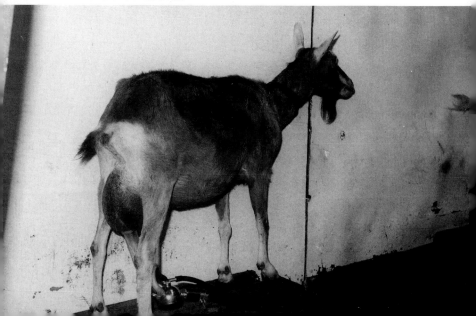

Kids feeding
Three different types of teat suitable for kids

Food and water bowls are best placed outside the pen to avoid wastage and contamination

Communally fed meat kids

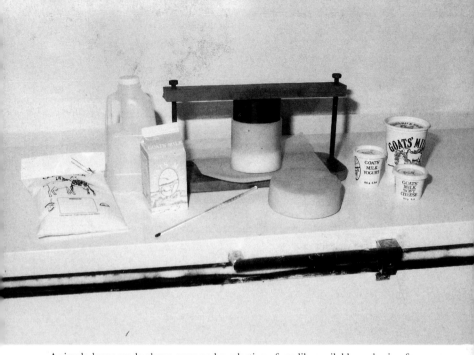

A simple home-made cheese press and a selection of readily available packaging for milk and dairy produce

Dosing a goat with a syringe

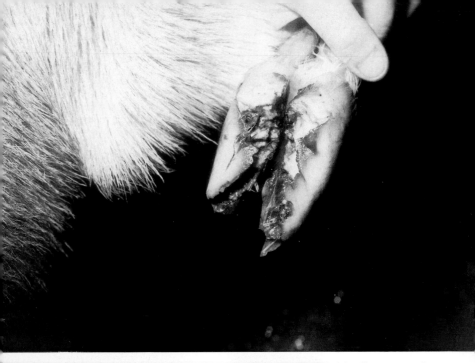

A hoof in urgent need
of trimming

The same hoof being
trimmed using the correct
foot shears

CHAPTER NINE

KEEPING GOATS HEALTHY

Although a large part of this chapter is devoted to illnesses that can occur if the goat is *not* healthy, the title was chosen to emphasise the importance of preventative medicine. As with all farm livestock, good husbandry, noticing symptoms promptly, cleanliness and lack of stress for the animals, are all of prime importance. Despite the best attention, things can go wrong, often through no fault of the stockman; therefore this chapter gives details of the symptoms and usual treatment of a number of the more common complaints that goats are prone to. Please bear in mind that this chapter is written from the point of view of the practical goatkeeper, not a qualified vet. Some complaints can easily be dealt with by the experienced goatkeeper, but others do need the vet. If you are in any doubt at all, at least telephone your vet for advice; he much prefers being consulted unnecessarily, than having to attend a dying animal whose owner has been trying home remedies for far too long. You will soon get to know which are the conditions that you can safely deal with, such as mild colic, foot rot, minor wounds, as well as routines, like vaccination and worming. There are some symptoms which make it imperative to call the vet urgently, such as total collapse of a goat, severe bleeding, broken limbs etc. Unfortunately, most illnesses are not so clear cut, and quite often the goat will simply seem 'out of sorts'. It is these conditions that I hope the following pages will identify and help to clarify those which need veterinary treatment.

As far as prevention is concerned, correct feeding at the crucial stages of growth, pregnancy and lactation, have been dealt with in the appropriate chapters and are of vital importance. Also not to be overlooked are routines like worming and vaccination, which will be dealt with later in this chapter.

FIRST-AID EQUIPMENT
There are a few first-aid items that all goatkeepers should have.

Some, such as antibiotics, would be only appropriate to the more experienced, apart from the invaluable purple gentian violet antibiotic spray for external use. This is available from your vet and is sold under many different drug company names. Because of the variations I will refer to it in future only as 'the purple spray'. Other essential items are needles and plastic syringes, wormers and vaccines, antiseptic cream, such as udder cream, as well as everyday tools like foot shears or a knife. You are bound to collect various things over the years as you learn to deal with more eventualities.

One essential, not to be forgotten, is a thermometer to take the goat's temperature before calling the vet. If you do this first, it will add to the information you can give him, especially in the case of a goat with vague symptoms. The temperature is taken by inserting the thermometer into the rectum, having first lubricated it (saliva will do). A goat's normal temperature should be between 102°F and 103°F (38.9°C and 39.4°C). A healthy goat can vary that much, but most have a temperature of about 102.5°F (39.2°C). A high temperature indicates some sort of infection, and a low one can be a very ominous sign, indicating the need for an urgent visit from the vet.

Another useful aid is a 10 or 20 ml plastic syringe for drenching. Old glass bottles used to be employed, but it is much easier and safer to give medicines by placing the syringe (without a needle!) in the side of the goat's mouth, and depressing the plunger slowly. Do not do it too quickly or the goat may choke, and for the same reason, only lift the head a little. Your thumb should be inserted into the gap between the teeth, as though putting a bit in a horse's mouth (see photo). Do not get bitten; goats' teeth are very sharp, especially at the back.

INTERNAL PARASITES

I have chosen to mention these first, for, in my opinion, there is more milk lost, and poor performance resulting from these than any other single factor in the goat's life. I am afraid that the small goatkeeper is often guilty of this failure to worm, and at the same time, the owner of farm goats, perhaps more used to cattle, may not realise how often goats need worming. Goats who are stall-fed are the most fortunate in this respect, and this is why so many larger herds prefer zero grazing.

Goats normally only ingest worms when grazing pasture contaminated with the larvae, deposited either by other goats or sheep. Therefore if you are grazing goats on land that has only been used recently by horses or cattle, you may be able to avoid worming for some considerable time. This assumes that all your goats were wormed before going out. If however, you have to use the same few fields for the goats every year, or have had sheep before, you will have to worm far more frequently.

Questions about worming, how often to do it, if at all, what brand of wormer to use, etc. always create a great deal of discussion and argument whenever goat people get together. There are those who do not believe in worming at all, and those who advocate doing it every month, come what may. There really is no easy answer as to how often, because circumstances vary so much. The type of land you have, the rainfall, the temperature, and whether the goats are grazing short grass or only browsing on heather, and other scrub, are all factors which have a bearing. If you are in any doubt, your vet will always test a dung sample for you and advise accordingly. I have to say though, that many vets still treat goats exactly the same as sheep, and do not realise that they react differently to some wormers and more importantly, do not develop the degree of adult immunity that sheep and cattle do. Because of this, it is necessary to worm goats throughout their whole lives.

Generally speaking if they are housed and not fed any cut grass that could be contaminated by goats or sheep, they should not need worming, but owners often like to do them once or twice a year to be sure. Any bought-in goat should always be dosed on arrival. Goats living on rough land, eating very little grass, but browsing on taller vegetation would need doing perhaps only twice a year in spring and autumn. Worm larvae do not normally live three feet up in a gorse bush!

Many smallholders reading this book will have the use of perhaps two or three fields which they may be able to alternate with cattle grazing or cutting for hay. Hay or silage aftermaths are considered safe, providing that the goats are wormed before putting them on it. This is where the difficulty lies; in a milking herd with daily sales, it is not practical to worm all the goats together because of the milk withdrawal time. This would leave you with none to sell for one to three days. Most of us find we have to compromise and do as many as possible over a period of days. This does mean that the clean pasture is no longer perfectly clean, but there will still be far less contamination than usual. Goats can live with a small challenge of worms quite happily, and it is only when this becomes heavy, that problems occur. If goats are all wormed on housing at the start of winter, in theory they should stay clear until spring when they go out again. I say 'in theory' because some wormers are better in this respect than others, so choose one which kills worms at all stages.

Another vital time for worming is around kidding time, as just about then, the worms in the gut put out a large number of eggs onto the pasture. In addition, the goat herself can be badly affected by worms at that time, and they are a common reason for poor appetite and reduced milk yield after kidding. If a goat has not been out at all since she was last wormed, this pre- or post-kidding dose will not be necessary, but should be given if grazing has continued during mild winter spells. Using the modern safe wormers it is quite in order to dose a goat directly after kidding, and we do it while she is still giving colostrum. Once the herd has been out grazing for three to four weeks on pasture that was used the previous autumn, they should then be wormed, unless the field was heavily grazed by horses or cattle, who 'clean up' the goat worms. How often to worm after that depends very much on whether the goats are able to be moved to clean land periodically. If not, it may be necessary to drench them every three to four weeks during the grazing season, and although this is expensive, it is in no way detrimental to the animals.

There is a limited range of wormers which are actually licensed for goats, but virtually all the modern sheep wormers are suitable. Probably the best of all is Panacur (Fenbendazole) which is especially appropriate as it is licensed for goats and very safe to use. It is usually given in the liquid form by means of a plastic syringe in the mouth. Medicines can be given in the feed, but it is not always easy to make sure that it has all been eaten.

Goat Nutrition's Multispec Bolus (Mebendazole) is made specifically for goats and comes in the form of a bullet-shaped pill administered by means of a plastic dosing gun supplied with it. It has a very short milk withdrawal of only twenty-four hours, and although more expensive than Panacur, the cost is offset against the smaller amount of milk wasted. It is also very safe, but the technique for dosing takes some practice. There are many other brands that can be used, some of which contain the drug Levamasole, which does not seem quite so effective for all goat worms, occasionally causing adverse reactions in the goat, especially when given by injection. It is not so suitable for the final autumn worming, because it does not kill the worms which burrow into the stomach lining at that time. These worms, a type of osteragia, lie dormant until the spring, when they can become active and cause parasitic gastro-enteritis.

Before leaving the subject, I must mention a product not intended for goats, but which we have used, at our own risk, several times, with nothing but good effects. It is called Ivomec (Ivermectin) and comes in a liquid form for sheep, or an injection for cattle. We used the latter, as it has the advantage of killing some external parasites as well. It is not suitable for milking goats as it has a very long withdrawal period for milk, but we have used it to good effect on male goats and dry 'rescued' goats in very poor condition and crawling with lice.

When working out the dose rate, for any wormer, read the instructions on bottles and packets carefully, and with the safe ones like Panacur, it is better to over-dose than give too little. Most adult goats weigh between 120lb (55kg) and 150lb (70kg), indicating a dose of 12.5ml of Panacur. A few goats, especially males, are bigger, and it is quite safe to give them the 15ml dose if in doubt.

I am often asked about the signs that indicate that a goat needs worming, and they are many and varied. There may only be subtle signs such as a goat failing to eat up all her concentrates, and while continuing to eat hay and greens, becomes more and more choosy with her normal milking ration. At the same time the amount of milk given may decline and she may become noticeably thin and rough in the coat. Because worms are of different types and live in various parts of the body, varied symptoms occur. It is not usually necessary to determine what type of worm or combination is the culprit, because all the modern anthelmintics are of a 'broad spectrum' type and cover most worms. If lungworm is present, the goat may be coughing and losing condition, and blood-sucking worms cause anaemia, which can be indicated by pale eye membranes. The droppings may or may not be abnormal in some way, anything from just slightly soft to profuse scouring. In the latter case, the goat will become very thin and weak and will actually look ill. It is likely, in that case, that the infestation has developed into parasitic gastro-enteritis, and it would be as well to call the vet. Needless to say, well-kept goats should not be allowed to get into that state.

Liver fluke

This does not seem to be as common in goats as in other livestock, presumably because they avoid the boggy areas that shelter the intermediate host, a small snail. If they are forced to graze this type of pasture, or if you have bought goats from a 'flukey' farm, then it would be wise to dose them in the autumn and again during the winter. Separate preparations for fluke drenching can be bought, or they can be combined with a wormer. Occasionally, this dosing can upset a goat, and for this reason avoid doing it around mating or kidding time.

If an animal has a severe fluke infestation, it is possible for it to die after dosing, but this is caused by the death of the flukes in the liver, rather than the drug. In this case, the liver damage is so severe anyway, that the goat is likely to have died whatever you had done. The symptoms are similar to those of a heavy worm infestation and in addition there may be a soft swelling under the jaw.

Coccidiosis

I have already given symptoms of this condition in Chapter 8 (see page 93), as it is kids who are affected, although all adult goats probably carry the parasite. It is most common in housed kids, particularly when large numbers are kept, but it can also affect outdoor grazed kids. In their case, the symptoms seen could well be a combination of worms and coccidiosis, and they will need treatment for both. The treatment for coccidiosis has to be obtained from the vet, and there are now several different medicines that can be used, some of which are far more effective than sulphamezathene, the usual treatment recommended in the past. Recently a preparation made for lambs called Deccox has come on the market. Inevitably, it has no licence for goats, but we have found it to be the best prevention and treatment of all, and can either be added to feed or put in their milk bottles. Many kids in the past had a disappointing growth-rate because of this

110

condition, and it is only now that it is getting more recognition from goatkeepers.

DIGESTIVE DISORDERS

Probably the most common digestive disturbance seen is scouring, or diarrhoea. The normal droppings from an adult goat take the form of dark brown or black pellets. A slight deviation from this is not necessarily a sign of illness, but may be as a result of lush spring grazing. If this type of dietary scour is seen and the goat is healthy in every other way, then do not worry about it, especially if she is eating and milking well. A goat's dung will always be more loose when on grass than when she is in on winter feed. Otherwise, a slight scour may mean that she has overeaten, or is due for worming. A more severe liquid scour, when the goat is looking obviously ill, could be a sign of something more serious such as poisoning, or entero toxaemia (see page 113). It is not always easy for a beginner to tell whether the degree of scour is sufficient to call the vet. As a general rule, I would say that, providing that the goat is still cudding, and at least eating hay or browsings, there is no need for urgent treatment. In such cases it may be that she has eaten something slightly poisonous and once it has all been cleared from her system, it is likely that she will be back to normal within twenty-four hours. If the scour persists, becomes more profuse and watery, the goat is in pain, ceases to eat or cud, or has a temperature and other worrying symptoms, obtain veterinary advice.

Scouring in kids has already been mentioned in Chapter 8, and it is always a condition to be taken seriously, as young animals can become dehydrated very quickly. As a general rule, milk feeding should be reduced or replaced by a calf electrolite powder. A simple medicine like kaolin can be tried, but if there is no improvement straightaway, call the vet or take the kid to the surgery. Older kids out at grass can scour badly from worms, even when the adults appear unaffected, and must therefore be wormed frequently.

Colic
This is a disorder sometimes seen in adults, but more often in kids. It is basically a bad stomach ache, usually with wind and bloating. The kid may be very distressed, have a swollen

belly, and sometimes constipation. She may throw herself about the floor, crying most pitifully, and as kids are very intolerant of pain, something must be done quickly. A first-aid measure, which is often enough to relieve the situation altogether, is a tablespoon of oil, with a teaspoon of bicarbonate of soda mixed into it. The oil can be medicinal liquid paraffin, or plain cooking oil will do if that is all you have to hand. It is best given by means of a plastic syringe, being very careful not to choke the kid. A kid of several months old would have a larger dose, as it appears to be quite safe, and can be repeated several times if necessary. The kid's belly should be rubbed to shift the wind, and if you can succeed in making her belch, that is a great help. An old-fashioned medicine like chlorodine often helps too, and I would imagine that if you had nothing else, baby's gripe water would help. If there is no reasonable improvement, the vet should be consulted. Colic in kids sometimes seems to have no cause, but in other cases it can be put down to her having gorged on concentrates or overfed on unaccustomed food, or lush grass. All feed changes should be gradual, and this applies equally to an adult goat, which can be treated if necessary with a larger dose of the home remedy recommended above. Often, walking her about will move the wind and make her feel better.

Bloat

True bloat seems to be comparatively rare in goats as opposed to other ruminants, although when having grazed all day, they often look 'bloated'. This is not the same thing though, and you have to bear in mind that the rumen of the goat is very large for her body size, and she is capable of packing in a large amount of roughage. This will of course make her look very fat, and the rumen will probably be noticeable on the left side. However, as long as the goat is not in distress, but lies down when you bring her in, and begins to cud, then it means that nothing is wrong, and by morning she will be completely deflated. Bloat occurs when this cudding and digesting process stops, and therefore the goat will not be cudding and is likely to be standing up, looking most uncomfortable. Drenching with oil or a special bloat drench may be enough to relieve the situation, otherwise skilled help is required, especially if her breathing becomes laboured.

Entero Toxeamia

This is a real killer, but fortunately, one that has an effective vaccine, which also covers related conditions caused by the clostridial bugs. These bacteria are present all the time in the gut and in the soil, and it is not known exactly what triggers them off to multiply rapidly, thereby producing toxins which kill the animal. In goats it usually comes on very suddenly; a goat who was perfectly normal, can be dead within twenty-four hours. The symptoms, if there are any before death intervenes, are extreme misery, profuse smelly scour, and later, convulsions and unconsciousness. There seems to be no effective treatment, as by the time the symptoms appear, the toxins are already at work. The course of the disease can be the same in kids, although death often occurs sooner and you may just find a dead kid, usually one of the best grown of a bunch. It was thought to be caused only by over-feeding concentrates, rich grass, or transporting animals, and it is true that these things and any other stress factors can trigger it off. However, many goats have died of it without any obvious stress factors being present and the only sure way to prevent it is by keeping up the vaccination. The vaccine to use can be purchased from agricultural merchants or vets, and the latter may be better for the beginner who may wish to have some advice on its use. Otherwise, if you are already used to using a clostridial vaccine on sheep, then use the product in the same way, except that goats should really be boosted every six months rather than twelve, as with sheep. Instructions on when and how to administer the vaccine are always included in the pack, so it is unnecessary for me to detail them here, except to emphasise that if pregnant goats are vaccinated at the right time, their kids will be protected for some months after birth. Products to use include Heptavax, Tasvax Gold, and any others of a similar type, and your stockist should be able to advise you. Some vaccines mention goats in the leaflet, and these are obviously ones to go for. Often an abcess will appear at the vaccination site, however clean and careful you are, and this is usually caused by a reaction to the vaccine itself. These lumps do not seem to bother the goat at all, and they may seem a small price to pay, compared with the death of a goat.

Poisoning

Because of the goat's natural inclination to sample any vegetable matter, they are rather prone to plant poisoning. Fortunately they are quite resistant to the effects of some simple poisons and a plant that would seriously upset another species can often be eaten safely by goats. Probably the most usual plant to cause more serious trouble is the rhododendron and its close relatives. The main symptom, unusual in ruminants, is vomiting. The severity of this and other symptoms depends on many factors, such as the time of year, the amount eaten, and how full of other food the goat was when she ate the plant. Goats vary in their reaction according to these factors, some showing no obvious illness other than perhaps a reluctance to eat for a day, while others are salivating, and vomiting particularly unpleasant green material all over the surroundings, crying out with painful stomach cramps, and occasionally, collapsing. We live in an area surrounded by rhododendrons and have had several accidents over the years. In my experience this form of poisoning, although dramatic, is not as often fatal as one is lead to believe. We have never lost a goat yet, and I have a suspicion that amateur efforts at drenching a very reluctant goat with various home remedies cause far more deaths from pneumonia than the actual poison does. If the goat is vomiting freely, most of the material will be ejected before harm is done. In many cases we have found that after having got rid of this offending material, the goat is better in twenty-four hours without any treatment. However, if the stomach cramps are very severe and do not seem to be lessening, obtain an injection of Buscopan from the vet, to relieve the pain. This is most effective in helping the goat to recover in her own time. It is also wise to give a multi-vitamin or B12 injection to protect the liver. I would not expect the goat to begin eating straightaway, but hay and water is always on offer. After about a day, she will begin to nibble straw and you then know that she is on the mend. Favourite foods such as brambles and ivy, or leaves, will often get her back to normal appetite, but offer fibrous food for the first few days, only gradually re-introducing concentrates. This poisoning has most effect on a milker, and she may well lose her milk, although if she is only ill for a short while, it should return as she eats properly again.

Yew is a very deadly poison, and goats should never be allowed near it, as there is no suitable treatment. The same applies to laburnum, and quite a wide range of other ornamental garden shrubs and trees. It is never wise to allow goats into a garden for this and other reasons, not least because of their destructive habits.

There are a number of wild plants which are poisonous, though rather uncommon, and because of this, are unlikely to grow on many farms. These would include hemlock, deadly nightshade, water dropwort and thorn apple. Woody nightshade is more common, but rarely causes death, although goats do eat it. Some poisonous plants are unpalatable to goats, and are therefore never touched. In this category I would place foxglove, which I have never known a goat to eat. The excellent BGS leaflet, 'Wild Food for Goats' also lists a number of poisonous plants to avoid.

Ragwort and bracken are both common and poisonous, although goats never eat bracken unless deprived of normal food. Ragwort is particularly palatable when wilted or in hay. Because it is so easily pulled up by hand, there is no real excuse for smallholders to allow it to proliferate, as a few minutes hand pulling every day will soon remove it from small fields and banks.

It is possible for goats to be poisoned by other substances such as weed-killer or plants that have been sprayed with it, rat poison and various chemicals found on farms. The most common culprit is lead. Nearly all old paint contains lead and goats are particularly vulnerable because of their habit of chewing wood. Goats should never be allowed near old painted wood, but if you have the slightest suspicion that lead could be causing illness, then call the vet at once. Prevention is *much* better than cure though.

BREEDING PROBLEMS AND THOSE ASSOCIATED WITH KIDDING

Pregnancy Toxaemia and Acetonaemia (also called Ketosis)
I have grouped these conditions together as they are very similar and have basically the same cause, the former being seen in the final weeks of pregnancy and the latter after kidding. They are both metabolic disorders, brought on by an imbalance between the energy intake from food and the amount going out. Although it can occur in thin goats that are inadequately fed, it is more frequent in goats who were allowed to become over-fat in early pregnancy. The goat with pregnancy toxaemia becomes more and more sluggish and lazy, eating less all the time. Concentrates are the first food to be refused, but later roughage as well is only nibbled and the goat will die unless proper veterinary treatment is given. Sometimes it is necessary to induce kidding, and this may result in a recovery. The best prevention is a gently increasing ration of

high energy food during the final six weeks of pregnancy. At the first indication that all is not well, further trouble can sometimes be prevented by feeding foods such as sugar-beet pulp and flaked maize, or giving sugar in the form of glucose or molasses.

After kidding, ketosis can be prevented by these same foods, but sometimes the first indication that a goat is ill is the refusal to eat concentrates at all. Her milk then decreases and she begins to lose weight alarmingly. Good grass or other green food is said to be a preventative, therefore the condition should be more common in housed herds. However, reluctance to eat concentrates can be caused by worms, and this would obviously only apply to grazed herds. Sometimes a pear-drop smell can be detected in the milk, urine or breath with this condition, and this is a sure sign. If giving sugary foods does not improve the goat's condition within a few days, then veterinary advice is vital.

Failure to show oestrus or to hold in kid when served
The former is not necessarily a problem with the goat, but often one of the owner failing to notice the signs, or expecting all goats to come in season as early as September. In these cases, housing the goat next to a male will usually do the trick. If this fails, any goat who has not come in season by the end of November should be seen by a vet, as should one who is served repeatedly and fails to hold to the service. A lutenising hormone injection may be suggested when she is next mated, providing that she is returning at the proper intervals. Goats who come in season irregularly, or who seem to be in season permanently are more difficult to treat, and are not often successfully mated. Obviously the male goat used must be fertile, and providing that other goats are in kid to him, then he can be presumed so. It is always worth trying a different male for difficult breeders, as occasionally another one will 'click' with her. Some male kids are infertile or have retarded development, and these should be culled. Any male kid who is not serving effectively by six months is suspect, although Anglo Nubians are sometimes a little more backward than the Swiss breeds. A kid should not be expected to serve a goat who is far too tall for him, although if he is keen, then the use of sloping ground may help. Unwilling, very fat or awkward goats are best served by an experienced strong male, although there is nothing to be gained in forcing a goat to stand if she is not in season. A

slight degree of unwillingness though especially if she is wagging her tail at the male, is not necessarily a deterrent to a successful mating. Goats are very fertile animals, who usually become pregnant as long as they are mated around the correct time. Having made a few attempts, an experienced stud male will lose interest if the goat shows that she is really not in season, although a keen young one will keep trying longer!

False pregnancy or cloudburst
For some reason, goats appear to be more liable to this condition than other animals. Goats who are not mated regularly every year, and overfat goatlings are particularly susceptible. It is always difficult to tell whether a goat is having a real, or false pregnancy, except by some of the pregnancy tests. She may have been mated, but it can happen to an unmated goat, who stops coming in season and whose belly grows very large. She may not dry off her milk or if a first kidder, may fail to develop an udder. Quite often she will go well past the kidding date, and then may discharge a large amount of water (the cloudburst), and behave as though she had kidded. Sometimes the water is discharged as a trickle over a period of days or weeks. Afterwards there may be a slight bloody discharge, and eventually she may come in season again, if it is still within the breeding season. In future, it is wise to mate such a goat at the beginning of the breeding season.

Milk fever
This is not a fever at all, but is caused by a sudden demand for calcium, usually directly after kidding, although it can come on later during the lactation, sometimes as a result of stress. The symptoms can be vague, such as a stopping or slowing of contractions while kidding is in progress, bloating, failure to cud, staggering, and finally, collapse. This is an emergency, requiring immediate attention. If you are experienced with dairy cows and know how to deal with the problem, you can administer the calcium yourself. Otherwise, call the vet at once and explain the situation. Recovery after prompt treatment is usually rapid.

Metritis or womb infection
This may follow an assisted kidding, but can occur when everything seemed to be normal, and may be caused by a small piece

117

of retained placenta. The infection responds well to antibiotics, if treatment is started in time. The symptoms include extreme misery, high temperature, unpleasant discharge, and sometimes mastitis as an added complication. Veterinary attention is essential as goats can die very quickly without treatment.

Prolapse
Some goats, when heavily in kid, can be seen to have a small part of the pink vaginal wall protruding from the vulva when lying down. If this is only slight, and goes back into place when the goat stands up, it may be better to leave well alone if she is not far off kidding, and her surroundings can be kept clean. The vet may prefer to put a stitch in the lips of the vulva, and of course this stitch will have to be cut when the first signs of kidding begin. A goat who has had this problem once is liable to repeat the performance next kidding, so you have to decide whether to keep her, but do bear in mind that some goats prolapse only when carrying triplets or more.

Prolapse of the womb
This only occurs after kidding and is a much more serious matter, for which the vet must be called without delay. While waiting, do not fuss around the goat unnecessarily, keep her as still and quiet as possible, and if it can be done without disturbing her too much, place a clean sheet under the displaced organ. Keep all other goats well away, because if the womb should be trodden on, it could be fatal. Plenty of hot water and soap will be needed by the vet, as with so many obstetrical emergencies, so should be ready for him. This condition is fortunately very rare.

Abortion
It is reasonable to assume that if only one goat aborts, it is often just one of those things, but if several do, or very premature live kids are born, then you probably have an infection in the herd, possibly contracted from sheep. Because there are so many different diseases that can result in abortion, you should consult the vet who will wish to take away samples. Pregnant women should not handle any of this aborted material, or assist in premature kiddings, as some of these diseases can pass to humans.

As well as infections, serious digestive upsets such as poisoning, severe stress such as worrying by dogs, and malformations of the foetus, can all result in abortion, and any one of these may well be the cause when only one goat is involved. Often there is a retention of the afterbirth and antibiotic treatment may well be needed.

CONDITIONS AFFECTING THE UDDER

Mastitis

Most farmers with dairy cows are familiar with this condition. It is caused by many different bacteria and can result in varying degrees of illness. The mildest from the goat's point of view, but one that is often difficult to treat, is sub-clinical mastitis. There are rarely any symptoms, except perhaps less milk than expected, an uneven udder, low butter-fat, or an unusual taste in the milk. In this case, the vet will ask for a sample and will test the milk. If bacteria are present, antibiotic treatment will probably be suggested. A goat who has had mastitis during the lactation will benefit from having dry-cow tubes inserted in the teats when she is dried off, which will often clear up a long-standing infection. Remember, that any goat with chronic mastitis is a danger to the rest of the herd, and her milk should not be sold.

Occasionally goats do have a very few clots in the milk resulting from her having banged or bumped her udder while at play, or escaping from the field! If no bugs are found to be present on testing then no treatment is needed.

More obvious forms of mastitis result in a hot painful udder with clots in the milk, greatly decreased yield and sometimes general signs of fever and illness. Probably the most dramatic form, which can result in the death of the goat, is gangrenous mastitis, also known as black garget. It usually flairs up very suddenly, sometimes affecting only one half of the udder which becomes hard and hot, the skin having a strange reddish-mauve hue. The milk, if you can call it that, is foul smelling and dark red. The goat is usually very miserable with a high fever, and even if treatment is started at once, she may die, but in any case is likely to lose part of her udder. Frequent massaging and stripping, with hot cloths applied, may help to aid the vet's treatment. After a day or two, the skin of the udder turns purple, then almost black and stone cold. By now the goat may be feeling better in herself, as the infected tissue is dying and separating off. This part will rot and actually fall off after a while, after which the goat recovers, and the wound heals surprisingly well with the aid of the purple spray (see page 106) and fly deterrent. Because the goat suffers a good deal, and maybe is left with half an udder, it is often recommended that she should be put down as soon as it is diagnosed. Just occasionally only a small portion of tissue is affected and the goat may be worth keeping. Goats with half an udder are often suitable as housegoats.

Prevention of all varieties of mastitis is better than cure, and keeping the goats' surroundings and lying areas clean and dry will help a great deal. Udders should always be handled carefully and milking machines never left on too long. Injuries to the udder or teats should always be treated seriously as this is the easiest way for infection to gain access. Mild skin scratches such as those caused by brambles or thorns rarely seem to lead to trouble, and an application of soothing antiseptic udder cream such as Capritect is sufficient. If the wound is more severe, especially if caused by barbed wire, it will need very thorough washing followed by a generous application of the purple spray, which is ideal for this job. We find that if the spray is applied as soon as possible after the injury, it prevents infection altogether. However, if inflammation does occur, or the milk is affected, then the goat must be seen by the vet. If the injury is serious enough for the milk to be leaking, then it will have to be stitched, and antibiotic cover given to prevent the mastitis which is sadly almost inevitable following a deep udder wound. Not all stitching operations are successful in stopping the leak, and some goats have to be culled later after all. Prevention of such wounds, by adequate fencing, is the answer of course.

After such a wound has been stitched, we have found that healing is improved and speeded up by the use of the juice or liquidised purée of comfrey leaves. As this is difficult to apply to a wound where bandaging is not possible, a wad of the purée can be held between the hand and the wound while you are milking. As the udder has to be handled for milking anyway, the goat suffers no extra stress. Milking badly injured teats is difficult but vital, and even when the goat is normally machine milked, hand milking is appropriate.

Pink milk
Sometimes a goat is seen to have pink milk, or blood in the milk. This is not necessarily a sign of infection or mastitis, but can be

as a result of a blow, or because of the pressure in the udder when a goat is newly kidded. It is the equivalent of a nose-bleed, and usually as unimportant. Small capillaries break and bleed into the udder, and usually, providing that there are no disease bacteria present, it will clear up in a few days. We find that it pays to milk such a goat very gently by hand, without any massaging or stripping out, three times a day, if that is possible. This milk is obviously unfit for sale, but can be given to pigs, dogs or cats. If the blood is allowed to settle to the bottom, the top half of the bucketful can be acceptable to kids or calves.

Oedema
Immediately after kidding, a goat will sometimes have a very congested hard udder, which does not yield much milk, and yet does not feel like mastitis. It is caused by a fluid retention and congestion, and will gradually soften up after a few days of gentle massaging. Hot cloths are also said to help, as is very rapid hand milking. The goat is not ill with this condition, and what milk there is, is quite normal. Usually the udder will soon show signs of softening, sometimes in one part of the udder first, and within a week or so, should be perfectly normal and milking well. If not, the vet should be consulted.

Maiden milkers
Although this is not an illness at all, it is relevant to this section, because the condition worries many people new to goats, and a goat can be ruined if not dealt with properly. Goats are so naturally compelled to milk, that they often come into milk as unmated goatlings or even as kids. It usually happens in the spring and summer, and very often, the udder only develops and milks on one side. This is nothing to worry about, and normal udder development will come on both sides after kidding. It is most important to check the udder frequently, and if it becomes full, a little must be milked out. Some goatlings only need to have a little milk taken off every few days, and others become so full, that they start milking full time, yielding as much as two or three pints a day. Once the goat is being milked regularly, this milk can be used as normal. Many goats have had their udders ruined because their owners did not realise that they needed milking. Chronic mastitis can result if such goats are not milked, and they may be found to

be useless after kidding. If the maiden milker is only a kid, just relieve the pressure a little as and when necessary to prevent the udder from becoming tight. No harm will come to a goatling who milks during her second summer, and it will probably prevent her from putting on a harmful amount of weight.

Few people other than those involved in showing, know that stud males can have this problem. They actually develop udders, or large teats, and have to be milked to prevent mastitis, just like goatlings. This is not a joke! It really happens to well-bred males from very milky families, especially when rather overfed for showing. I hasten to add that these are perfectly normal fertile males, and are not hermaphrodite goats. Needless to say, this milk is not used!

Spotty udder

Goats often suffer from spots on their udders or teats, and these are rarely anything serious, just a nuisance. They are normally referred to as 'goat pox', and are caused by a number of different bacteria and viruses. They will usually go away of their own accord, perhaps with the assistance of udder cream or the purple spray. The latter is especially useful if the spots come to a head and contain pus. If the condition persists, you should consult your vet. Although cleanliness helps to prevent them, some goats seem very prone to spots and in such cases they could be an allergy.

EXTERNAL PARASITES AND SKIN DISEASES

Lice

These are commonly seen, and most goats have them to some degree, particularly when housed fully during the winter. They do not live in the surroundings, but actually on the goat, and so are therefore picked up in the first place from another goat. When the infestation is slight they probably do little harm, but it is easy for them to get out of hand if the goat is not in the best of health. Lice are often combined with a worm infestation, which can be serious as both conditions can result in anaemia. This will be apparent from the goats' eye membranes, which will be very pale. Other signs of lice are a rough coat, covered in ruffles where the goat has been scratching with her front teeth, bald patches around the neck, and a scurfy skin. The fawnish pink lice can be seen in a good light on the coat. A dusting of general animal louse powder will usually control them for the time being, or shampooing with a suitable lotion if the weather is mild. Goatkeepers are starting to make use of new sheep preparations, which can be poured onto the back, and these are excellent for keeping goats free from lice for some considerable time, and appear to have no side-effects. Although these preparations do not usually state a milk withdrawal time after use, it is suggested that the first milk following treatment be discarded, or used for stock. Ivomec injection is a very effective insecticide, but not suitable for milking goats (see Internal Parasites, page 109).

Mange
There are several different forms of this complaint, some much more serious than others. A common one is leg mange, seen in housed goats. This will very often disappear on turn-out in the spring, but meanwhile the legs can be washed with Alugan (an insecticide and fungicide). Because some forms of mange are more difficult to treat, any skin complaint that does not respond to washing with Alugan should be seen by a vet.

Ringworm
This fungus disease is not very common in goats, although they can certainly get it, usually from other livestock like cattle. You could catch it yourself, so be careful how you handle affected goats, and wear rubber gloves if touching the scabs. Goats usually get this in a mild form, having one or two patches on the ears or face. Sprays are not a very effective treatment, and your vet will supply you with a powder to add to their feed, which if eaten, is very effective. However, goats, unlike most other animals, are unwilling to eat medicated feed. Although ringworm is not really harmful, it looks most unsightly and is not a good advertisement if you have stock for sale.

Orf or contagious pustular dermatitis
This is a much more troublesome complaint than the former, and quite common among both sheep and goats. It is easily transmitted to man, and can result in unpleasant skin trouble, so avoid touching any suspect spots on goats' mouths without rubber gloves. It is often contracted from sheep, particularly tame lambs which have been bought in to drink up surplus milk.

Goats usually have it in a rather mild form, showing scabby spots at the corners of the mouth and sometimes on the lips and nose. Because it is caused by a virus, there is no effective treatment, but spraying with the purple spray prevents the spots from becoming infected and spreading. By this means the scabs may be limited in number and disease may not spread to the entire herd. It is most important to avoid getting it on the udder, as the spots there seem to be much more troublesome. In sucking kids, it can affect both the dam's udder and the inside of the kid's mouth, which is serious as the kid will be reluctant to feed and the goat's udder will become over-stocked. There is a vaccine, but it has drawbacks which the vet will explain to you.

Fly problems
Although in theory goats could suffer from warble flies, possibly of the deer variety, it is rarely heard of. There is no compulsion to treat goats for this or for sheep-scab mite. Ordinary goats certainly do not suffer from scab, but it may be that Angoras can be affected. It is unlikely though that such valuable animals would be allowed contact with undipped sheep.

I have never heard of a goat being attacked by fly maggots in the way that sheep can be, and they are not usually troubled much by flies in the way that horses and cattle are. This is probably because the lack of body smell makes them uninteresting to flies, unless they have an open wound. In this case the goats must be protected with a suitable fly repellent ointment or spray. The de-horning of adult goats, which has to be done occasionally, should not be carried out during the hot months, because it is very difficult to keep such large holes from becoming infected. This operation is best done in the spring or autumn.

MISCELLANEOUS PROBLEMS

Feet
Providing the goats' feet are examined and trimmed frequently, they have very little trouble if they are kept on hard ground. However, in Britain, the ground is often far from hard and dry, and those owning large herds are not always as attentive as they should be with preventative trimming. Not only owners of larger herds, but people who keep only a few goats often neglect the latter's feet dreadfully, and there is certainly no excuse in that case.

When you are buying goats, foot trimming is likely to be one of your first tasks. If a hoof has been badly neglected, attempt to get it back into shape gradually, as it will not be possible to achieve this all at once. If the side horn has come away and dirt is packed inside, cut all the loose horn off and clean out the space, afterwards spraying with purple spray. All bad-looking or rotten material should be cut away, otherwise the rot will spread into the sound horn. It is likely that the goat will still limp after you have done this and sprayed the foot, but in a day or two she should begin to walk sound. If not, it could be that the infection has worked right into the hoof. Unless you are experienced, it would be best to let the vet have a look at it and decide what further treatment is needed. He may cut into the infected place and let the pus out, after which recovery is often rapid, but antibiotic injections may also be needed.

Goats sometimes suffer from sore white skin in between the toes, normally known as scald. It is easily noticed though, as even in the early stages the goat goes very lame. At this stage a generous spraying is usually enough to nip it in the bud before it spreads any further. Occasionally, something resembling a flat corn may develop in between the toes, which also makes the goat very lame. In my experience this condition does not respond well to any home treatment, and it is usually necessary for the vet to cut it out.

Prevention of foot complaints is best achieved by the provision of ample dry bedding and, if possible, a concrete area for exercise. Goats should really be kept off the land when it is very muddy.

Navel ill (sometimes progressing to joint ill)
This is the result of germs gaining access through the navel cord of a young kid. The first sign is a swollen navel, often with pus and an unpleasant smell. The kid may also have a high temperature. Navels should always be treated at birth with a suitable antiseptic which usually prevents trouble occurring later, but if it should happen, a further spraying may be all that is needed to clear up a mild infection before it has taken hold. If neglected, it can lead to joint ill when the infection gets into the body and can result in swollen joints and lameness. This will need veterinary attention so, as usual, prevention is best.

125

Hernia

Kids sometimes have an umbilical rupture, which is usually only small, but may be very large. Although it is feasible to repair a small one, it is rarely worth it unless the kid is very special. It does not seem to affect their growth rate or condition at all, so it is often best to leave well alone and rear the kid for meat.

Teeth

Goats grow their teeth in just the same way as sheep, gradually replacing the first ones until the set is complete at about four years old. Like sheep and cattle, they have none at the top front, and nip off food by the action of the lower teeth against the hard pad at the top. The teeth are often used as a chisel, to remove bark from trees and branches. As a goat ages, these front teeth may become loose and fall out, but this is by no means as usual in goats as it is in sheep. A fourteen-year-old goat may still have a perfect set. Goats can still be productive when the teeth have gone as long as they are not called upon to eat very short grass. Just occasionally, at the time when young goats are changing their teeth, their gums become rather inflamed and painful. This makes them refuse food, and they stand about, looking as though they have toothache. The face may also swell a little. It is very difficult for the vet to do anything other than perhaps give antibiotics, or a painkiller.

Abcesses

These can occur anywhere on the body as a result of a small puncture wound or thorn, but most often occur on the cheeks when some sharp piece of food has worked its way through from the inside while the goat was eating, resulting in an ugly swelling on the goat's face. Strangely enough, these lumps seem to cause the goat little or no discomfort, and I feel they are best left alone to develop. Usually, the abcess will come to a head, and once it has burst can be cleaned and sprayed, after which it will heal quickly. I would certainly not wish to lance one of these,but there is no harm in encouraging it to come to a head by bathing in hot water. Abcesses are also very common at the vaccination site, not necessarily as a result of a dirty needle. Sometimes they come to a head and can be cleaned, but otherwise just leave them alone.

Eye trouble

Although, on occasions, a goat will have a running eye caused by a foreign body, most watering eyes are similar to the 'New Forest eye' of cattle. Watering is the first sign, and the eye is often half closed. If not treated, the eye will become cloudy and a spot may appear in the centre. This should be treated with an ointment given to you by the vet, or he may have to inject into the eye surround. Treatment is effective if started in time, otherwise the animal may go blind. It is easy to spot the symptoms in a milking goat or housed kid, but not so easy in a herd of Angoras running free, so observation should be thorough, especially in summer.

Pneumonia

Although this can easily occur in goats, it does not usually spread through the entire building, in the way it can with calves. Usually just one animal is affected, often after a change of weather from hot to cold, or cold to damp, or it may be brought on by some stress factor such as moving from one farm to another. To begin with the symptoms are rather vague; I call this stage pre–pneumonia, with the goat looking very miserable, reluctant to move or eat. If nothing is done, laboured breathing and perhaps coughing will follow, with sometimes a nasal discharge. The temperature is usually up at this stage, but can become low if the goat has been ill for some time before being observed. This is one illness where I would always use antibiotics, as, especially when given at the earliest stages, they effect a complete cure. Pneumonia can also be caused by careless drenching, and I always prefer to avoid pouring large quantities of liquid down a goat, as they are very unco-operative when compared with other animals.

Heat stroke

This seems an unlikely complaint in this country, but it can happen, especially to a tethered goat who cannot get out of the sun. Black goats in particular are affected, and will pant excessively, before collapsing. The goat must be moved out of the sun as quickly as possible, and cooled off by sponging with cold water. It can also lead to pneumonia (see above).

Urinary stones

Most commonly seen in male goats, whether adult stud goats or castrated kids. There are various theories as to the cause, but the condition certainly seems to be connected with feeding high levels of any concentrate food, and failure to drink enough water. Stud males' water buckets become very dirty from the immersion of their soiled faces and beards, so must be cleaned frequently. Any male goat seen trying to urinate without success should be seen by a vet at once. In the case of a kid being reared for meat, immediate slaughter would be the answer, as most treatments are not very successful. In the case of males kept for stud, any treatment may render him impotent. If such an animal is not killed or treated quickly the bladder could rupture, leading to a slow and painful death.

SERIOUS DISEASES

Johnes disease

I have left two of the most worrying and serious diseases to the end, as neither can be treated. Johnes disease is probably more common than was once thought, although it is not simple to diagnose and a post-mortem examination may be necessary. The main symptom is a gradual weight loss over a period of months in an adult goat. She normally continues to eat well and only in the final stages will you see scouring, although the dung may have been soft before this. The disease contracted by the kid, invariably from its mother, but may not show itself until many years later, and remains in the soil for some years. There is no cure or treatment, but the vet is the only person to advise you if you should be unfortunate enough to get it in your herd.

Caprine arthritis encephalitis (known as CAE)

This is a very worrying new disease which has only reared its head in recent years. At present it is very rare, and opinions vary as to what should be done to keep it that way. If you wish to start off your herd with CAE free goats, you should insist that they all be blood tested before purchase. However, this is no real guarantee, because the virus can be slow to show in the blood, and the herd you bought your goats from may have only just begun to be tested. Goats from a herd that has been tested every six months for perhaps a year or two should be safe, but one cannot be one hundred percent sure. It is likely that by the time you read this, new regulations will be in force covering showing and testing, and the sale of untested goats. To begin with, this would only be feasible with pedigree goats. There is a voluntary accreditation scheme similar to the Maedi–Visna scheme for sheep as the two diseases are very closely related. At present there is no vaccine or treatment.

In adult goats the most usual symptom seen is a swelling and lameness in the joints, chiefly the knees, but, even more worrying, is the fact that it often affects the udder, causing gradual loss of yield and hardness of the tissue. It is most easily passed on by means of the milk, straight to the dam's kids and other kids if the milk is mixed. It is possible to try to control it in a herd by not feeding any milk from infected dams to kids, but there are other ways of contracting it as well. Fortunately it is quite safe to use the milk for human consumption as the virus affects only goats and sheep. Although most goats showing signs will be mature, there is a form which can affect the brain of young kids, which so far does not seem to be present in this country. The British Goat Society will supply details of the testing scheme to anyone interested.

ALTERNATIVE OR CONVENTIONAL TREATMENT?

Throughout this chapter you will have noticed that I often refer to antibiotics or other drugs. While I am fully aware of the public concern about the over-use of these powerful medicines, and indeed share it, I feel that they are essential in many cases. Severe infections like pneumonia and acute mastitis respond very well to quick treatment with antibiotics, and it is worth bearing in mind that goats tend to just give up and die if they are ill for a long time. I would hate to think that I had deprived an animal of efficient treatment, just because of a personal principle. There is an increasing use of homeopathy for veterinary use, but it is important that you either have a very extensive knowledge of the principle yourself, or have a vet who is prepared to treat in this way. Homeopathy does work very well in the right hands but there are very few vets at present conversant with its use. There is little harm in your experimenting with non life-threatening or trivial complaints yourself, but there is a legal requirement to get proper veterinary help for a suffering animal. Until there are more vets interested in alternative treatments, you really have no choice but to make use of modern medicine. I certainly do not advocate the use of antibiotics on a routine basis; they should be kept for specific cases, such as retained afterbirth, or an infected foot that is giving a goat a lot of pain.

The gentian violet and antibiotic spray that I often mention is a good prevention of infection in any kind of wound and speeds up the healing process. It is of course only applied externally, and as such only treats the desired area. Antibiotics given by injection or through the teat have a withdrawal period for the milk and meat from that animal, and these must be adhered to rigidly. Cows' milk used to have a very bad name in this respect and in the goat world we have to rely on our own integrity to keep our milk pure. This is most important, as many people who drink goats' milk for medical reasons have multiple allergies and can have a serious reaction if the milk is contaminated.

Occasionally I come across people who are so against 'chemicals' that they will not worm their goats or rid them of other parasites. This is very shortsighted and cruel to the goats. We all keep goats in very unnatural conditions, ie on lush grassland, or confined areas, when in the wild they were designed to roam for miles over rocky and sandy terrain. This is why they have little resistance to worms, and, having domesticated goats, we must use unnatural means to keep them healthy. Modern wormers are excellent, in that they act on the parasite itself without affecting the host. Garlic is not an effective vermifuge, and many goats have become badly infested while eating their garlic faithfully. The only way to keep goats without worming them is never to allow them to graze the same pastures, or keep them inside all the time.

Goats remain very natural and healthy animals compared to some other farm stock and it is our duty to keep them that way.

CHAPTER TEN

GOATS' MILK PRODUCTS

The first thing everyone thinks of when considering goats' produce, is the milk, pure and simple, but there is a wide range of products that can be manufactured. In addition to milk products there is also kid or goat meat, the skin, and the fibre from the Angora or feral goat.

Many goatkeepers begin by wanting to sell only milk, but soon find that they are being asked for yogurt and soft cheese at least. Because these are relatively easy to make, do not take a great deal of time or need expensive equipment, you may wish to consider them.

I would suggest that, to begin with, you experiment with a small quantity of milk, for which the following recipes are suitable. Should you decide to expand later, and invest in a cheese vat, or yogurt incubator, the basic grounding you will have had in small-scale production will be invaluable. I would strongly recommend that anyone contemplating cheese production on a large scale should attend one of the excellent courses available. The tuition on offer is usually given by a trained expert, often from a farm institute or agricultural college. To find out about such courses, contact your nearest agricultural college or Agricultural Training Board officer.

It should be emphasised that while it is perfectly in order for you to make some cheese for home consumption in your kitchen, this will not satisfy the Health Inspector when you begin selling. It is necessary to have a separate room for the purpose, which is likely to be next to the dairy where you do your milk packing, and washing up. I will explain some of the regulations covering production in Chapter 11, but for now I will concentrate on the recipes themselves.

One small item of equipment that is essential before you begin is a plain glass thermometer, either a dairy one or a cheaper wine-making one.

CHEESE

Cheese starter

A cheese starter is a bacterial culture, these days often purchased in a dried form, which has to be made up before use, or propagated in fresh milk to render it active. If a starter is not used, the cheese will be very variable, which is undesirable in a product intended for sale. It may well have either an unpleasant 'goaty' taste, or very little flavour at all. The starter provides the proper cheesey taste, and once you have used one, I can guarantee that you will taste the difference. It is necessary to know how to propagate and increase the starter, otherwise you will only be able to make a few batches of cheese from each bottle or sachet of starter. Most packets will have instructions, otherwise you can use the following method, which is very simple.

Take a large thermos flask, preferably wide necked, and about 1³/₄pt (1 litre) capacity, wash well and sterilise with dairy hypochlorite or Milton. Then rinse with boiling water, both to warm the flask and remove the chemical. Heat 1³/₄pt (1 litre) (or the flask's capacity) of new milk to about 160°F (70°C), and keep at that temperature for about fifteen minutes to heat-treat it and make sure that there are no unwanted bacteria present. Cool to 80°F (27°C) or the temperature advised on the packet, and add the starter, stirring until it is dissolved. Pour into the warmed flask, seal, and keep the flask out of draughts or excessively cold places for twenty-two to twenty-four hours. When you open it up it should smell cheesy and slightly acid. This made-up starter can then be divided into small pots or bottles, sufficient to make one batch of cheese each. Put one in the fridge, where it will keep for up to one week, before which time it should be re-propagated with fresh milk, or used to make cheese. The remainder can be frozen, and although this starter looks watery when defrosted, the bacteria are still there, ready to go to work on a fresh lot of milk, and the cheese will turn out just as well. It is difficult to be exact about the amount of starter to use for cheese making, as providing that the milk is kept warm, the bacteria will go on growing in it until they have turned it all cheesy. For most purposes a tablespoon

132

per gallon is a good average. This type of starter will suffice for all sorts of cheese, but as you get more adventurous, you may wish to try the different cultures obtainable from specialist suppliers.

You will also need cheese rennet, now available like the basic starter, either by post from the goat and dairy equipment firms (see page 167) or from agents. Ordinary junket rennet is quite unsuitable for hard cheese, but it can be used for some soft ones.

You may have noticed that you have a choice of real animal rennet, obtained from the lining of calves' stomachs, or what is known as 'vegetarian rennet', a substitute. Either of these is suitable, and I can honestly say I have not noticed a great deal of difference in their performance, but if you have a number of vegetarian customers, you would wish to take this into account.

Lactic cheese

This is a soft, creamy white cheese that is usually eaten on crispbread or biscuits, but also makes an excellent cheesecake ingredient, and can be used in many recipes.

Heat $1^1/_2$gal (7L) of milk to 160°F (70°C) (the quantities can be reduced or increased as desired). Cool to 80°F (27°C). Pour into a large stainless-steel or Dairythene bucket, add about two tablespoons starter, cover and leave in a warm place for twelve to twenty-four hours. The temperature should not rise above 80°F (27°C) but the hotter the place, the shorter time you need to leave it. This milk should now smell cheesy, and once this has occurred, heat up another gallon of milk to 160°F (70°C), cool to about 100°F (38°C) and stir in one teaspoon cheese rennet diluted in six teaspoons of cold water (this dilution helps distribute the rennet through the milk more easily). Immediately pour the renneted milk into the previous day's cheesy brew, and the whole can now be kept at ordinary room temperature. Again leave for twelve to twenty-four hours, until it is well set like junket, and the yellow whey can be seen floating on the surface. Ladle out the curds carefully into a large cloth supported inside another bucket, tie with clean tape or string into a bundle and hang up to drip. For goats' milk it is better to use old white sheet material, which is easily boiled and sterilised, rather than muslin. Goats' milk curd is very soft and may pass easily through the larger mesh of muslin. After twenty-four hours' dripping, or less in hot weather, change the now more dry curd into a fresh bag, muslin being ideal at this stage, and hang again. Once the cheese is no longer dripping at all, take out of the bag and fork in about one teaspoon of salt. At this stage you can add chopped fresh herbs such as chives, or other flavouring. This cheese will keep refrigerated for about a week, but freezes well in little pots. If it is for sale, these must be correctly labelled (see Chapter 11).

BASIC CHEESECAKE MADE WITH LACTIC CHEESE Naturally you will have your own favourite cheesecake recipes, but this is a very simple and quite inexpensive one needing no cream.

Make your usual biscuit-crumb base with digestive biscuits and half their weight in melted butter or margarine. Press into the base of a spring cake tin or tinfoil dish.

Take 1lb (450g) cheese, sugar to taste, normally about two tablespoons, and add two egg yolks. Beat together with an electric mixer. Then beat in ½lb (225g) of any kind of fruit pulp, either cooked or raw, add one sachet of gelatine dissolved in a little water or fruit juice and finally fold in two stiffly beaten egg whites. Pour the mixture gently onto the base. Decorate when it is set.

All sorts of fruit can be used in this recipe, including the special additive-free fruit pulp in tins, made especially for yogurt making. Use fresh fruit like strawberries and raspberries, cooked fruits like apples and blackcurrants or a tin of frozen concentrated orange juice, with mandarins for decoration. The eggs can be omitted, or a little yogurt added; the variations are endless.

Hard Cheese

I feel I must include the method for making a simple hard cheese, although I have to say that it is not really worth making, being very time consuming, unless you are able to specialise and concentrate on making it in a fairly large way, with all the proper equipment and cheese vats. However, you are bound to be asked for it by your customers, and it is likely that you may wish to make a little for your own use in any case.

If possible, use a double saucepan with a water jacket around it, as this will minimise the risk of scalding the milk while heating. This cheese can either be made from milk that has been heat treated first, or from fresh milk straight from the goat, which

134

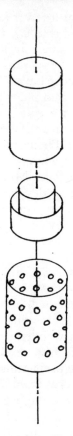

A cheese mould, showing the position of the follower and wooden follower

I think produces a better cheese. The milk should be at about 80°F (27°C) when you begin. Add a tablespoon of starter to 1 gal (4.5L) milk. Leave in a warm place, or with warm water in the outer pan for about three-quarters of an hour. Add half a teaspoon of rennet, diluted with six teaspoons of cold water, and stir gently throughout the milk for a few seconds. Leave to stand for three-quarters of an hour or until the milk is set and the whey visable. Then using a long knife, cut the curd into slices and then cubes. You can buy a special knife for this purpose, but otherwise any long stainless-steel knife will do. With *very* clean hands, gently stir the curds and whey while

135

slowly raising the temperature over a period of about one hour, until it reaches about 100°F (38°C). It is not necessary to stand over it for the whole time, but you do have to be nearby to stir frequently and check the temperature. Turn off the heat and let the curd, which will now have a rubbery look, sink to the bottom. Pour off the whey and place the curd, in one piece, into cheesecloth and leave it in a colander for about half an hour. The room should be warm and the curd covered to prevent it from cooling too much. Then cut the curd into about three pieces to allow some more whey to run out. Leave for half an hour, cut and turn it over again. Meanwhile, prepare the mould and press. All sorts of home devices can be used to substitute for a real cheese press, even just heavy weights, but better is the kind of simple screw device illustrated (see photo on page 103). Plastic moulds are easily available now, and are made in various sizes.

Crumble the curd as though making pastry, then sprinkle the small pieces with a little salt and press it all into the mould, filling it right to the top. You will be surprised how much it goes down when pressed. If your mould has a plastic 'follower', this goes on next, otherwise a wooden block has to be used which should be covered in cling film, to keep the cheese clean. The mould should stand in the press on a cane or plastic cheese mat to help drain the whey. Screw down the press just a little to start with and tighten gradually throughout the day. The next day the cheese should be turned and pressed from the other side, harder if possible. On the final day, turn the cheese again, and press as hard as possible for about another twelve hours. When the cheese has been taken out of the press and mould, leave it on a wire rack in an airy place to dry out, turning it every so often. If you do not mind mould on the surface you can complete the maturing process naturally in a cool larder. I find that wrapping the cheese in a piece of white kitchen paper, changed daily, helps the drying process and keeps dust off. If you wish to keep your cheese for some months, or want a more professional look, it is simple to coat the cheese in wax which will seal it and keep the mould out. Cheese wax is best kept permanently in an old saucepan ready to melt in order to dip the cheese. This wax obviously gives a more professional look to cheese intended for sale, and I would like to repeat that a proper course should be attended if manufacturing cheese is going to be an important part of your venture.

YOGURT

This is the product that almost all goatkeepers make at some time and it is very simple, once you have mastered the art. It is a little like making bread, in that it is necessary to experiment with temperature and method to get it right in your conditions. People often complain that their yogurt is too thin. To some extent, goats' yogurt is always going to be thinner than cows' because of the softer curd, but it should not be runny. To start with, you need a milk of good butterfat and solid content, for which the milk of Anglo Nubians is renowned. Also, milk produced from about September until the end of the winter is always thicker than summer milk. It is possible to thicken your summer yogurt by adding dried goats' milk. Never use ordinary dried milk unless you are not offering it for sale, or have labelled it to make it plain that some cow produce is present. This labelling is not only a legal requirement, but essential for those with allergies.

Do not worry if you do not have a proper yogurt maker, those thermostatically heated boxes containing small pots; most of the best yogurt is made in homemade incubators. The aim is to keep the milk as near to the required temperature as possible, while the bacteria are growing. For this you can use an insulated picnic box, previously heated by putting in a box of very hot water. It is also possible to use a large flask, but the curd breaks down when the yogurt is poured out, which rather spoils its appearance.

I prefer to incubate and make the yogurt actually in the pots as this gives a better look to the finished product. If you are intending making it on a large scale you can buy proper yogurt incubators that hold dozens of pots. These have the appearance of a fridge which, instead of being cold inside, is warm. It is quite feasible for a handy person to make one of these from a disused upright freezer, using a light bulb for the heater. It will be necessary to experiment with the size of bulb and time kept switched on, but because the cabinet is so well insulated, it stays warm for some time after the heat is switched off. It should be fairly easy to obtain a freezer which does not work.

The correct temperature for incubation depends on the culture used, but it is between 100°F (38°C) and 120°F (49°C). We find the higher temperature best. Dried yogurt starter, like the cheese starter, can be obtained, but unlike the latter, cannot be frozen satisfactorily. Fresh yogurt has to be made every few days to keep it active but you should be able to continue making yogurt for some weeks, just by using one pot from a batch to start the next one.

Method for making yogurt
Firstly, bring the milk to the boil (this reduces the water content and thickens the milk a little). Then cool to the required temperature. Meanwhile, if you are going to make the yogurt in the pots, put about half a teaspoon of yogurt or starter into each pot. Alternatively, the starter is added to the milk while it is still in the saucepan. Pour the milk into the container or pots and incubate. Leave in the incubator for about six hours, after which time, it should be ready. The incubator is then opened and the yogurt allowed to cool a little before refrigerating. Ideally, yogurt should always be sold within a week of manufacture, but it does actually keep much longer than this and is still suitable for home use when at least two weeks old.

To make flavoured yogurt, either add some fruit at the end when the yogurt is served, or use a proper fruit pulp made for the purpose. Goat Nutrition make an excellent product for this purpose, which consists of thick fruit in a tin, with no preservatives or artificial colour. Because it is sterilised, it can be put into the individual pots, starter and milk added, and the whole incubated together. Fresh fruit should never be used this way, because wild yeasts and other undesirables could interfere with proper incubation, and produce an unpleasant or even dangerous product.

CREAM

Goats' milk is naturally homogenised, which means that the fat particles are very small and distributed throughout the milk instead of rising readily to the top. This makes hand skimming very difficult, although it can be done if you are able to leave the large wide bowl needed in a cool place for twenty-four hours. Hand skimming is not practical for commercial quantities, and you would need a separator, which is rather expensive, although there are a few firms now reconditioning second-hand ones. If you are intending selling cream on anything but the smallest scale, you will need an electric separator. All separators are tedious to clean

138

and re-assemble, but at least an electric one spares you the hard work of turning. It is best to put the milk through the separator while still warm from the goat, although it can be heated and done later, if it has cooled. To make it a viable proposition, the cream has to be sold for a fairly high price, and some good use made of the skimmed milk. This can be made into a true cottage cheese, using the same recipe as for lactic cheese, although the finished product will be much drier and more crumbly. The skim can, of course, be used for animal feeding, although in these days of anti-fat mania, you may be able to sell it as low-fat milk!

CLOTTED OR SCALDED CREAM

Since goats' milk is always white, clotted cream will not have the same golden colour as real Devon or Cornish cream, but it is still delicious and can be used in the same way as the real thing. It is very easy to make on a small scale for home use, but I doubt if it would be commercially viable.

Leave a large flat bowl of milk in a cool place for twenty-four hours, then set it carefully over a pan of gently simmering water, on the cool plate of a solid fuel stove, or a very low gas flame. It can be left like this for between half an hour and one hour according to taste. The longer it is heated, the more of a caramel flavour it will have. Return the pan to the cool place carefully, without disturbing the wrinkled surface, for a further twelve hours, after which the surface will have stiffened, thus making it easy to skim. The remaining milk will not have lost all its cream, unlike mechanically separated milk, and is particularly suitable for cooked milk puddings.

ICE CREAM

Once you have cream, any ice cream recipe can be used. This one is very simple, and ideal for the light fluffy cream of goats' milk. It can easily be made with a small quantity of hand-skimmed cream.

Whisk $^1/_4$pt (150ml) cream until it is very fluffy, then whisk in 4 level tablespoons icing sugar and a few drops of vanilla essence. With the whisk on a slow speed, add two previously stiffly beaten egg whites, and if desired, a trickle of red fruit juice with the final stir to make a ripple effect.

Freeze at once as quickly as possible. This is a type of ice cream

139

that does not need whisking again half way through the freezing process, as the egg whites hold the air in suspension.

Ice cream is one dairy product of which sales are still increasing, but it requires a high capital outlay to set up a business to make it for sale.

It is possible to make butter from goats' cream, but it will be pure white unless you add oleo butter colouring. A separator would certainly be needed and the butter would have to be sold for a high price to make it worth making at all.

KID MEAT

Nowadays, lean meat is very popular, and kid meat, being one of the leanest of all meats, is gradually becoming more accepted by the public. The fat on a goat is distributed quite differently from that on a sheep or a cow; instead of being within the tissues, and therefore impossible to cut right out, goat fat lines the inside of the carcass in the form of a suet-like hard white fat, very easily removed. There is also a considerable amount of this suet round the kidneys, and this indicates that the animal was well fed, although she may have had a thin appearance. In very fat goats such as barren goatlings, this suet can be several inches thick, filling much of the body cavity. It is not difficult to see why such goats are difficult to get in kid!

The aim should be to slaughter kids before this fat starts to build up, and in practice this would be from three to six months old, when they weigh 45lb-80lb (20-36kg). At this stage the meat is very tender, lean and mild in flavour and can be cut up and cooked like lamb, which it resembles. If uncastrated males are used they should be slaughtered no later than about five months of age, before they begin to smell. Because kid meat is not yet bought and sold by normal butchers, most has to be sold direct to the customer. This demand is increasing, and many of us hope that eventually the butchers and public will realise what they have been missing all this time!

Before the meat can be utilised, the kid has of course to be killed. You should not do this yourself unless you are skilled in slaughtering, even if it is for your own use; there are regulations covering the actual slaughter and the method used. The best way is either to take the kids to one of the abattoirs that are equipped to slaughter goats, or call in a private licensed slaughterman. There are quite a number of such people in country areas, who are usually employed in the trade, and do private jobs in their spare time. However, if you are intending selling meat, the kids must be killed at a slaughterhouse in order that the meat be inspected. For your own home consumption, this inspection is not necessary, and this is where the private man is so useful. A properly skilled operator will make a quick job of killing, and the kid will be dead before you can blink. He will usually skin and clean the carcass for you, leaving you to arrange the butchery the following day. Young kids do not need hanging for more than a day or two. You may have a local butcher who will cut it up, otherwise many goatkeepers do the job themselves, using a large hacksaw (with a new blade). We have a very good butcher who will make sausages for us and these are quite delicious, being very lean. There are endless possibilities, including burgers and mince. These manufactured products can also be made from older goats who have to be culled.

When cooking kid meat, remember that it is a very dry, although tender meat, and must be cooked slowly. Really hot roasting will make it shrivel up, and for this reason, it is best cooked in a covered roaster, or wrapped in foil to keep all the juices in. The lid can be removed for the final fifteen minutes or so. The addition of a little pork or beef fat while roasting adds to the succulence, and flavour can be enhanced by any herbs you care to use. Rosemary sprigs inserted into small slits in the surface are particularly good. For casseroles, a gentle cooking is again best, and the addition of some bay leaves makes it more interesting. You may well find that you prefer kid to lamb after you have tried it, as being less fat, it does not leave a greasy feel to the mouth.

Finally, on this subject, do not give names to meat kids for obvious reasons!

GOAT SKINS

Having had some kids slaughtered, you now have the skins to utilise. If they went to a slaughterhouse, you will need to make a point of asking for the skins back. They will tell you that these skins are of very little value, and if you try to sell them in the raw state, you will come up against a brick wall. Most of the hide dealers are just not interested and will only offer you a pittance, however prettily marked they are. There is a limited sale direct to the makers of Irish drums, and you may be able to track down one of these small businesses through a folk music club. Otherwise, it will be necessary to have the skins cured if you want to sell them, or indeed use them yourself.

There are several methods of curing skins at home, two of which are mentioned below, but if you have a large number of very attractively marked skins that you intend to sell, it is probably best to have them cured professionally. Home curing is very time-consuming and laborious, and does not usually result in such a good end product.

Goatskins cured with the hair on, especially when this is of an attractive pattern or colour, or is long and silky, make beautiful rugs for the home. Many people use them as chair backs or seat covers. We have them as seat covers in the delivery van. Those who would not wish to have wild animal furs are often quite happy with sheepskins, and would appreciate coloured goatskins as an alternative. As the male kid has to be killed anyway, it is best to make use of everything you can.

For those wanting to cure the skins themselves, then Katie Thear's little book *Home Curing* is excellent, describing several different methods to suit all skins. I find that the skins from all the meat kids are so time-consuming to cure that I prefer to send them to a tannery. It is not easy to find one willing to do small jobs, but you have to persist and telephone all the tanneries in your phone book, as well as ask other goatkeepers. Some advertise their services in *Home Farm* and *Smallholder* magazines. One problem is that it is difficult to send raw skins away, although they can easily be returned to you by post after curing. Skins can be stored for curing in several different ways, but I think the simplest and best is to put the fresh skin straight into the freezer in a polythene bag. They keep perfectly for many months in this way, but only if they were in good condition before being frozen. Traditional salt storing can be used, but you need large amounts of cheap salt and somewhere suitable to keep skins. In damp weather, the salted skins will run with water all the time.

If you have a small skin to do, such as that of a dead newborn kid, or one only a month or so old, then it is quite an easy job. The skin is so soft and small that it is simple to work in your hands, without becoming stiff.

Method for curing small skins (double the quantity for larger skins)
Mix one teaspoon each of salt and alum together dry, and rub all over the flesh side of the skin with your fingers. Fold the skin over once, skin sides together, then again, fur to fur. Leave folded like this in a cool place for four days. On the fourth day, open it out and lie it flat, flesh side up on newspaper. Twice at least, during the day, pull and stretch the skin both ways with your hands. Repeat on the fifth day, and on the sixth, peel off the outer layer of thin paperlike skin on the surface. This is the most fiddly and time-consuming part. The leather underneath will begin to look like white buckskin. Every day from then on, pull and stretch the skin frequently, also rubbing it up and down the edge of a table to abrase the leather and prevent it from becoming stiff. If you do this religiously, and do not neglect it even for a day, after about ten days the drying process will be complete and you will have a beautifully soft skin, with a clean white appearance on the underside. Moths will be your only problem, and these must be kept away. Small skins make pretty mittens or slippers.

Method for curing larger skins
This method is suitable for larger skins if you have time to spare.

Mis together the following chemicals which can usually be obtained from the smaller chemist shops: 4 gals (18L) cold water (soft, or rainwater for preference), $^1/_2$ oz (15g) borax, $^1/_2$ pint measure of dry salt and 1 oz (25g) sulphuric acid, added together in that order. Be very careful when adding the latter, which can be excluded if it is unobtainable. Having cleaned off the fat and fleshy bits from the skin, soak for between two and six hours in this mixture depending on thickness of skin. Make up a mixture of 2 gals (9L) soft water, 4 oz (125g) oxalic acid, and a 2 pt measure of dry salt and place the skin in this for at least two days.

Remove the skin or skins from the mixture and wring them dry without rinsing. Hang them up to dry. A dry, airy place is needed and the pulling and stretching procedure must be carried out as they dry. I do not feel that this method produces as good a skin as the tannery would, but the skin will keep and not decompose.

MOHAIR AND CASHMERE

I will refer again to the Angora and feral goats in Chapter 11 but here I would like to say, that for the enterprising goatkeeper who is a skilled home-spinner, the prospects are good. The fleece of the Angora and of some of the crosses, can be used profitably in the manufacture of mohair garments. These fetch a very high price when well made, and sell as quality goods. I would suggest that those interested in utilising this fibre themselves should obtain some spinning experience first and find themselves a spinning teacher. There is no doubt that profits can be made by selling any high-quality product of a rarity value direct to the public. The under fluff, or cashmere, from the feral goats is more difficult to handle and is usually spun with lambs' wool. The industry is in its infancy in Britain, and the openings are there for the innovator.

CHAPTER ELEVEN

PRODUCTION AND MARKETING

Although all the previous chapters have been aimed at those who wish to keep goats with the intention of establishing a profitable business, this chapter will give you some specific guidelines on how best this can be achieved. Commercial goatkeeping is becoming very popular, and, as a result, it means that every new herd owner has to develop and find his or her own markets against competition. Now, and for the foreseeable future, goat farmers have no Milk Marketing Board to buy and distribute their milk, and because of this, there is no point in setting up a commercial herd only a few miles away from an established one, with no thought for the marketing.

There are basically two alternatives: either you have to sell all your milk yourself, perhaps having made it into cheese, yogurt and other products, or you sell in bulk to a manufacturer.

SELLING BULK MILK

This option is very tempting, because it means that you can concentrate on being a goat farmer rather than a salesman. There are a few snags though; firstly, it is not easy to find one of these manufacturers just in your part of the country, especially if you live somewhere very remote. Another problem is that he may not be able to take all of your production, and you may find yourself still having to sell some elsewhere. You may have to deliver the milk to a distant collecting point, or if he comes to fetch it, he may not always arrive when expected. One of the worst worries, is that many of these small cheese and yogurt makers are inadequately financed and become insolvent after a while, leaving you with a herd that you may have built up just to supply them. Lastly, the price you have to accept may not be what you would wish for. Most bulk buyers pay between £1 and £1.50 per gallon. Bearing in mind the production cost of the milk, which I will refer to later, the lower price is only just profitable.

Despite all these disadvantages, if you can find a small factory to supply, and find them reliable, then this is a very good way of selling large amounts of milk. Try to find one that has been in business for many years and has a good reputation for prompt payment. Some definite arrangement should be made for delivery and payment. The payment ideally should be made upon their taking delivery of your milk, but should certainly be no later than one month.

There is no easy way to find one of these manufacturers, but the Goat Producers' Association may be able to help by putting members with milk to sell in touch with those needing it.

In Wales, there is a milk-drying factory producing dried goats' milk; at present it is the only one in Britain, but it would be possible for a group of producers to co-operate in developing this type of business. In Scotland there is a successful goat co-operative and I think that this is a good way forward for the smaller producer particularly. The problem in setting up such a co-operative venture is that capital is needed, and most goat farmers understandably prefer to spend available money on developing their own business. In addition, someone with a great deal of business expertise is needed to organise everything.

There are some firms offering contracts to goat farmers who are able to make curd, which is partially made cheese, for export. This is an excellent opportunity for the herd owner starting from scratch, as it offers a way to sell his entire production continuously. There are stringent hygiene and other requirements that have to be complied with, and a special curd incubating room will have to be constructed or adapted. The Goat Producers' Association will be able to supply addresses of the firms involved, to anyone interested.

SELLING DIRECT TO THE PUBLIC OR SHOPS

This section is for the producer who does not wish to tie himself to one outlet, preferring to have his eggs in many different baskets.

The production of a clean and wholesome product is of the utmost importance, and having perfected this, presentation and marketing must be carried out in a professional manner. Some marketing advice can be obtained from bodies like COSIRA, the Council for Small Industries in Rural Areas, and some councils have schemes for promoting local foods. The importance of hygiene and correct cooling, as well as storage of the milk, cannot be overstated. Although these things are important for all goatkeepers, the commercial herd has to be above suspicion. The Goat Producers' Association runs a clean milk scheme for its members who, providing their milk passes all the tests can use a special label on their packaging.

In the past, goats' milk has suffered from a bad reputation for being produced in a haphazard, amateurish way, and having a 'strong' taste. Unfortunately, this reputation is all too often deserved, and for some years now, both large and small commercial goatkeepers have been striving to correct this image. The taste of the milk is the most important aspect of all, for if you cannot get that right, the most palatial milking parlour and dairy in the world will not help you to keep customers. It is perfectly possible to produce clean and wholesome milk with the most basic of facilities, which the small-scale producer can easily provide.

For the present, goats' milk does not come under the Milk and Dairies regulations, like cows' milk, but it is misleading to suppose that there are no checks on its production. Although it is not considered to be milk, goats' milk and products are covered by food hygiene regulations and certain others, such as those involved with Weights and Measures. The Environmental Health Officer of the council is the official concerned with goats' milk, and I would advise anyone setting up a new enterprise to get in touch with the council first. New regulations concerning goats' milk are being discussed constantly, and if and when they do come into force, it is probable that they will still be policed by the local authority. It is likely that participants in the G.P.A. clean milk scheme will be looked upon very favourably.

With regard to the building of such structures as cheese-making rooms in particular, it helps greatly to ask their advice first, to make sure that what you are planning does come up to the required standard. It is not usually necessary to apply for planning permission if you are merely adapting an existing building on a farm or smallholding, and intend processing your own milk only. For new buildings, especially if near your boundary, permission may be needed. This particularly applies if you live in a National Park. It is always wise to check

147

these things with the council first, as mistakes will be very expensive to rectify.

ESSENTIAL MILKING AND PROCESSING FACILITIES

The area where the milking is carried out must be separate from the bedded area where the goats live and should have a washable floor and walls. It is not necessary to have a cow-type milking parlour if your herd size does not warrant it. The dairy, for handling the milk and washing up, should also be separate, and either lead off from the milking area, or be in a different building. It can even be a room in your house, though quite definitely *not* the kitchen where your own food is prepared. Some large, old-fashioned farm houses have a proper dairy and this sort of room can easily be brought up to date. It must have running hot and cold water, a suitable deep sink or dairy wash-trough, proper drainage including a floor drain, and washable walls and surfaces. You may also be asked to install a hand basin, but this may be overlooked if there is one nearby. This room will be used for cooling the milk and packaging it and should contain storage facilities such as the bulk tank or freezers. The milking machine parts can also be dismantled and washed in the dairy, and there should be storage racks for such items as milking buckets, strainers and the cooler.

If you want to make products from your milk, the authorities usually insist on a separate room, or at least a division in the dairy. In other words, you will need a place for milking, one for washing and packing, and another for manufacturing. It will naturally make for easier working if all these rooms are adjoining.

There is no requirement to pasteurize goats' milk at present. Because goats in Britain do not carry diseases like brucellosis and TB that can be passed to man, the authorities controlling cow production have never insisted on goat legislation. However, some producers find that the shelf life of fresh milk is longer if it is heat-treated, and do it for this reason. Many customers do prefer raw milk though, especially now that untreated cows' milk is very difficult to obtain. There is some evidence to suggest that 'natural' or raw milk does contain subtle properties not fully understood, which seem to aid digestion. However, if customers wish to heat-treat it in the home before giving it to young children, they should be advised not to raise the temperature above 160°F (71°C) because overheated milk undergoes changes in flavour and character.

If you have a number of customers who request pasteurized milk, or if you wish to prolong shelf life and avoid all risk of a goaty flavour, then you can install a small pasteurizer. These are now readily available from dairy supply companies, such as Fullwood and Bland (see page 167) who will instruct a potential buyer in its use.

PACKAGING

Unless you are selling all your milk to a manufacturer, in which case he may provide you with containers, proper packaging is vital. It is most important that goats' milk is presented in attractive containers and must never be sold to the public in old bottles. If you use one of the purpose-made cartons or bags, all the necessary information about the quantity and contents is printed on already, and you only need add a label with your name and address. This label is not actually obligatory if you sell direct from your farm or market stall.

Milk cartons, which are made from poly-board or waxed card, are probably the most attractive packing, but by far the most expensive, costing up to 8.5p each, depending on quantity bought. They do not need any special tool for sealing, a plastic clip to apply by hand is supplied, although they can be heat-sealed if prefered. Heat-sealing may be best if you are selling large amounts of fresh milk every day, when a packaging and sealing machine can be employed. These are obtained through the carton suppliers. However, as most producers sell much of their milk in the frozen form, hand applied clips are quite satisfactory. Cartons will stand upright in the freezer while being frozen, and are less liable to damage while being stored than plastic bags which are the most usual alternative. They also travel better, and when packed tightly together, will remain frozen for quite long periods in transit.

Often used in larger herds are machines for making, filling and sealing milk bags from a continuous tube of plastic, but the smaller producer will use the ready-made bags. These are the most popular form of packaging, although some shops do not like them, and insist on having their milk in cartons. Bags need very careful handling when frozen, do not display well, and customers find them awkward to defrost and decant into a jug at home. Against this is the considerable advantage that they are very cheap, only costing about three pence each or even less when bought in bulk. An additional benefit is that all the goat equipment firms supply bags in various designs, by mail-order or through stockists, so that they are easily obtainable. After careful filling with a measured pint, they are closed by means of heat with a small sealer. The cheap imported sealers are not now easily available, but there are at least two better ones sold by goat supply firms. These are British made and cost between £40 and £60.

If neither of these options suits you, then disposable plastic bottles are made in various sizes from 1 to 4 pt. The larger ones have screw caps, but the pint ones need a capping tool. They are made blank and unprinted, and need a descriptive label affixed. These bottles are best for liquid milk, although they can be frozen. There is a temptation to re-use them, but this should be resisted, because as they are intended to be disposable, they are not easy to clean and sterilise. Glass bottles are not really practical unless you have sufficient customers for a traditional milk round, when you can ask for them to be returned every day. They also need special facilities for washing, and taking everything into consideration, disposable containers are easier and cheaper in the long run.

FROZEN MILK

A great deal of goats' milk is sold frozen. This is possible because of the very small fat particles which do not readily rise to the surface, thus making the milk naturally homogenised. Goats' milk customers tend to be scattered over a wide delivery area, therefore making a daily fresh milk round very difficult to justify. They soon become used to having a week or a fortnight's supply in one go.

Certain rules have to be followed faithfully if the milk is to defrost perfectly for use. Firstly the milk should be cooled as described on page 52, and then frozen as quickly as possible directly after milking. Although some authorities feel that it is necessary to have a commercial blast freezer for this, we find, as other goatkeepers do, that providing you do not overload it, a large domestic deep freeze will do the job. It is a good idea to have more freezers than you think you need to avoid putting too much fresh milk in one cabinet. The freezer must be running efficiently at a low temperature and the milk must be sold before it is three months old. In practice, we like to turn over all our milk much faster than that in case there is a build-up in a shop causing further delay before it is sold.

Another important point is to avoid letting the milk defrost, even slightly, during transport to the shop or customer. A refrigerated van is needed for large amounts, but satisfactory results can be achieved for short journeys by means of insulated boxes. These can be homemade if necessary, lined with polystyrene. Cardboard boxes and newspaper are adequate for short journeys in winter and for customers taking their milk straight from the farm to their freezer.

If these rules are disregarded, or the customer keeps frozen pints out of the freezer too long, the re-frozen milk will separate and look most unpleasant when finally thawed out for use. This milk is not harmful in a bacterial sense, having undergone a mechanical breakdown in the milk structure, but is obviously undrinkable and only suitable for animal use. This problem should be avoided by strict attention to the rules but if a customer should complain of separating milk, she must be recompensed if it was not her fault. Shops must be educated on the care of the milk, and your transportation must be swift. The customer should be advised to defrost the milk slowly, preferably in a fridge, although a microwave oven is suitable if the milk is needed quickly. *Hot water thawing must never be used under any circumstances.*

MAKING AND SELLING PRODUCTS

At some stage you are going to have to decide which products, if any, you are going to make. Once you begin selling milk your customers will ask for other things such as yogurt and cheese. I hope I have given you some ideas for making these in Chapter 10. All goods must be packaged attractively, and there are yogurt and cheese pots made in different sizes and matching the milk bags and cartons. There is an enormous range of cheeses that can be made from goats' milk, but many of the recipes are carefully guarded trade secrets, although I have given you the basic recipes. Cheese can be hard, pressed, semi-hard, moulded or soft. For hard cheese an eye-catching label is a great selling point, and soft cheese can be packed into pottery jars or little wooden boxes. Small cheeses can also be packed in an original way, and will then command a higher price. In addition, there are all sorts of variations such as the addition of herbs and flavourings, special finishes, coloured waxes, and of course, the 'mouldy' or blue cheeses although the latter are, I feel, the most difficult to produce consistently on a small scale. In fact all sorts of other products can be made including mousses, sweets and fudge; the possibilities are endless for the enterprising goatkeeper.

As I suggested in Chapter 10 if you are interested in cheese-making it is a great help to attend a proper professional cheese-making course. If you are intending to develop a really interesting and unusual cheese, a great deal of time and effort must be spent on research into getting it just right before you launch it onto the market.

There are a number of distributors throughout the country who specialise in local delicatessen products and have many outlets in suitable shops. If you can put yourself in the hands of one of these, most of your marketing worries will be over, although you still have the responsibility of producing a consistent product all the year round. Otherwise, you will get a higher price by selling direct to the retail outlets yourself, but naturally, in this case all your time and transport has to be taken into account.

Goats' milk and the goods made from it can find outlets in a variety of shops such as wholefood shops, delicatessens, dairy shops and specialist cheese shops. In addition there are all sorts of outlets in tourist areas, who may be pleased to take your wares in summer only, when you have a surplus.

When approaching a shop, take a sample of the products and a full price list, and explain fully how the goods must be stored and the likely shelf life. Incidently, this period of time is often dependent on the temperature of the refrigerated counter, so ask about this if possible. Generally, for most things, the lower the temperature, the better. Give a dummy carton to display if all the milk is to be kept in a freezer, and one for the window as well if the shop wishes.

THE BENEFITS OF GOATS' MILK

Nowadays there is a tendency for goats' milk to be sold as a special food, rather than as a medicine for sick people. This used to be a very effective angle in the past, when all goat literature was sprinkled with case-histories of people who had made a miraculous recovery from a variety of ills through drinking it. These days, it is better not to make so many claims in this way, unless you can prove them medically, but simply emphasise the known *facts* about goats' milk.

There is certainly an increasing number of people with cows' milk allergy, and there is no doubt that most of them are far better and healthier when taking goats' milk instead. Although the actual fat percentage is similar to that of cows' milk, there is some evidence to suggest a slightly lower cholesterol content, and this will appeal to many customers.

Because of the very fine fat particles, goats' milk is much more quickly digested than cows' milk, forming a soft curd which only remains in the stomach for a short time. This is of obvious benefit to anyone with digestive problems, and the lightness of the milk can be a great relief to sufferers from indigestion. Little is really known about the properties that seem to aid digestion, and which are destroyed on pasteurization, but it is true that clean, raw milk certainly does seem to suit the digestions of some people best.

There has been a lot of publicity on the need for calcium in the diets of certain people; growing children in particular need it for good teeth and bones and it is also lacking in the diet of some older women who may go on to develop osteoporosis (softening of the bones). Goats' milk has a plentiful supply of calcium and other minerals and vitamins as well.

All these are factors that enable goat producers to sell more of their goods, but I think the most important factor of all is the excellent light taste of goats' milk with no trace of greasiness. This makes it especially suitable for adding to tea and coffee, and also for making sauces and custards.

Seize any opportunity that you can for good publicity, such as taking a stall at country fairs and fêtes. Cold milk tasting near the goat tent at agricultural shows is very popular. This milk should, of course, be supplied and dispensed by a commercial goatkeeper, and not taken from the goats being milked in the tent at the show, when hygiene and proper cooling are impossible.

Finally, the most obvious outlet of all is from your own farm gate, and a great deal of goats' milk is sold in this way. Do have an attractive notice, not a piece of cardboard in the hedge and ask the council if it is possible to have another on the nearest main road. Farm shops are very popular these days and you do not need planning permission if you are selling only the produce from your own farm.

REGULATIONS

There are quite a number of regulations concerning weights and measures and labelling that will affect you. The best person to ask for advice in these matters is your local Trading Standards Officer. Put simply, these rules require that packaged food must be labelled with a true description, such as 'full fat cheese', and a list of ingredients if applicable, together with the correct weight, usually in both grammes and ounces. Because these regulations are changing all the time, it is inadvisable for me to attempt to explain them in detail. Different councils also tend to interpret them differently.

There is a move afoot to label many foods, including dairy products, with their total fat content. This is going to make life very difficult for the goatkeeper, whose milk quality changes at different stages of a goat's lactation and with even small changes in feed and weather. Unlike cows' milk, ours does not become standardised after having passed through a milk factory.

Unless you are selling only milk, which is measured, not weighed, you need to have proper scales, tested regularly by the Weights and Measures inspector. Domestic kitchen ones will not do and there are a few firms who re-condition old shop ones. The address of such a firm may be found in your local yellow pages under 'Scales and weighing equipment'.

GOATS' MEAT

As well as all the milk products, there is also goats' meat to consider. This may either be a by-product from the dairy herd, or a separate enterprise involving Angora or Cashmere goats. To obtain a good price for this meat it is necessary to sell direct to the public, or at least to high quality restaurants, possibly those of Greek or Italian origin.

You may also be asked for kids killed for Halal or Kosher consumption, but many goat-owners are not prepared to submit their kids to anything other than the pre-stunning method of British slaughter. Be very careful if asked for live kids, as they may be sent very long distances to other parts of the country for religious slaughter.

The goat meat business is still in its infancy and marketing is difficult, although the extreme leanness of the meat is very much in its favour these days.

COSTINGS

In order to estimate the likely income from a herd of dairy goats, it is necessary to work out the probable costs you will incur. Firstly, there are the capital costs involved in setting up the herd and these will be very variable according to your circumstances. Naturally, if you already have buildings that can easily and cheaply be adapted, your setting up costs will be far less than if building from scratch. Many farms have an unused dairy and milking parlour that could be adapted at a low cost. A simple bucket-unit milking machine will cost at least £500 new, and a milking parlour and pipeline system a great deal more. Second-hand equipment will be a lot less of course if you can find it. Freezers will have to be bought, and these vary a great deal in price according to where you buy them. Second-hand ones can often be found for between £50 and £80 but they should be checked over to make sure that they are really working efficiently.

There are a great deal of small items like strainers, churns and cheese-making equipment that you may need. Reference to one of the dairy supply catalogues will provide you with the current prices for these items, and several different catalogues should be consulted as prices vary.

Discounting the building, the highest cost to be incurred will be that of the goats themselves. At present, milking goats seem to be in very short supply, and are not easy to come by cheaply. As a consequence, the price for good stock is rising rapidly and in addition, silly prices are being paid for inferior goats. An average purchase price for each milking goat could be about £70, but you could have to pay much more. These days it is unlikely that you will find many for sale under £60, and better-quality animals could be £100, so you should budget for at least £70 per goat.

After the capital costs, there are of course the day-to-day running costs for your herd. Although it is impossible to give you exact figures for things like rent or mortgage, electricity, water charges and interest on capital, I can give you some guidance as to likely feed costs. From these figures it will be possible to work out the cost of milk production.

Feed Costs

It is difficult for me to give you exact figures because even feed outgoings vary so much from herd to herd. So much depends on whether you can produce your own forage at low cost, or will have to buy in expensive hay all the time. Concentrates normally have to be bought in, unless your farm grows barley or oats, in which case a protein feed may be all you have to buy to balance the cereal. Your bedding straw costs would also be minimal on this type of farm. The highest costs are incurred by zero-grazed herds, but these are likely to milk consistently and will have no parasite problems leading to heavy worming costs. The following figures are a rough costing for goats out grazing in day time for about seven or eight months of the year.

Each goat will need about half a ton of hay or the equivalent in silage. Bought hay may cost about £60 per ton, depending on the part of the country you live in and its availability. Concentrates fed at an average of 2lb a day over the year, cost about £65 when using goat mix. On top of this figure of £95 so far will be the midday sugar-beet fed for about five months, costing £4.50. In addition you will have to take into account all the other variable costs like electricity, bedding straw, vet bills, fertilizer, and even your labour!

This feeding régime, costing about £100 per year per goat, is suitable only for goats yielding between 150 and 200 gallons per year, which is a reasonable yield to begin with. Goats are unlikely to yield to their full potential until they settle in with you. If the milk is sold for £1 per gallon, which I feel to be the lowest price you should even consider, this will give you a margin over feed only costs of £100, for a 200-gallon goat. This represents an income over feed costs of £2,000 for 20 goats. Naturally all other costs have to come out of this, but if you are selling your milk at a more sensible price of £1.50 per gallon, this immediately increases income by 50%. You should certainly be able to command this much by selling packaged pints of milk, even having deducted the packaging costs. If you are using bags rather than cartons, this cost will be lower, thus giving you a higher price.

Special cheeses and yogurt fetch a much higher price than

milk, even taking into account the fact that you have to make it. A small yogurt sells for about 20p, and so, having deducted the cost of the pot at about 5p, then the income per gallon is £4.80. Before you become excited at the prospect, it is unlikely that you will be able to sell your whole production of milk in this form.

It is a perfectly worthwhile proposition for a small farmer to keep a herd of perhaps twenty to thirty goats, but it is improbable that it would be able to provide his whole income. A goat enterprise of this size can easily fit into an existing farm or smallholding, as you will see from the following chapter, perhaps thereby enabling a small farm to be viable when before with conventional animals it was not. Bear in mind that you have to actually sell all the milk, and this is where some difficulty can arise.

PROVIDING A STEADY SUPPLY OF MILK

It is a fact that, under natural conditions, all goats kid in the spring, so are at peak production during early summer, and are at their very lowest in December to March, which are the months of highest demand, particularly for pints of milk. The demand increases during winter mainly because everyone else's goats are going dry at this time, especially those belonging to very small goatkeepers who sell a few pints during the summer to neighbours. Their customers then come into the shops to buy their milk in winter, and up go your sales, only to drop again as soon as you have plenty to sell in spring. It is not an easy situation to resolve, as frozen milk does not store perfectly for long enough to be put away in summer for late winter use.

Most commercial herds deal with the problem in a combination of ways, such as running through the very best milkers to give a level yield throughout the winter, kidding some out of season, and seeking summer-only outlets. The latter may be tourist-trade places like caravan sites and beach shops, or small ice-cream makers may be interested in making some goats' milk ice cream. This is one product that is certainly in very short supply at present.

Even if you sell bulk frozen milk only in one or two gallon blocks to a cheese-maker, he is likely to want a reasonably steady supply all the year round, and may wish to have a formal agreement with you to this effect. When you are a serious goat farmer, it is almost essential to resort to out-of-season kidding, although many people have a reluctance to interfere with the animals' natural cycle, other than by running a male goat with the herd at all times. Marketing this uneven production is the most difficult problem that the budding goat farmer will come up against, and one which he will have to resolve himself. I'm afraid there really is no easy answer.

ANGORA AND CASHMERE GOATS

The Angora goat which is very fashionable at the moment, but very expensive, is another possibility for those not wishing to keep a milking herd, and also for crossing with dairy goats to produce saleable grading-up Angoras. Pure-breds have been fetching anything up to £7,000 and even first crosses making a £100 or more for females but prices are falling. These prices cannot be justified by their crop of mohair, which at best will bring in about £60 a year. It is their rarity value that is resulting in these high prices, and they are bound to become more realistic in the end. Anyone wishing to set up a herd in the near future will need a great deal of capital, but if you could buy just one male, it is possible to grade up through dairy goat crosses, to get pure Angoras in about six generations. This male would have to be exchanged each year or two with one from another breeder, to obtain fresh blood. The main income is from the hair, shorn twice a year and yielding about four or five kilos per year. Castrated males can be kept on, simply to produce this fibre, but it is doubtful whether the price received would cover their feeding costs, although they would require less food than a breeding goat. The crossbred male kids are normally slaughtered for meat, but not before a potentially valuable fleece of a cashmere type fibre is shorn. Not all first crosses produce this fibre, but a good rug could be made from the skin. All female crossbreds are of course retained for upgrading and many produce a saleable 'cashgora' fleece which is the name given to the fibre from these goats.

Angoras are normally kept like a flock of sheep, with all the kids running with their dams and it is not normal to milk them. One big difference from sheep, is that like all goats, they dislike rain, and must always be provided with shelter and good food inside in case of bad weather. Sheep poly tunnels have been used very effectively, but any simple field shelter will suffice for summer. It is probably necessary to bring them right inside during winter though, especially in the wetter parts of the country. Routines like vaccinating, foot trimming and worming must be attended to, but unlike sheep, they do not have to be dipped.

At the moment, a large number of dairy type goats, or indeed any female goat, for that matter, are being used as recipients for embryo transfers. Pure-bred Angoras are induced to produce far more eggs for fertilization than normal. These are removed and transplanted, two at a time into the recipient females. This artificial process is very new, and of course, has to be carried out by trained veterinary staff, and as such, it is very expensive. Some goatkeepers are not happy about using goats in this way, but there is no doubt that the recipients are very well cared for, at least as long as they are carrying the precious offspring. I doubt if so many will be transplanted once the number of Angoras in the country has increased greatly, and they no longer have the rarity value and such artificially high prices.

The feral goat, which is the closest thing we have in this country to a 'wild' goat, is kept for producing cashmere and meat, as well as for the hill farm improvement schemes. To my mind they would be a doubtful proposition financially unless your farm is in a true hill area and has acres of rough, under-used pasture. Goats do have the ability to improve such pasture, by removing the tougher weeds and encouraging the growth of finer grasses and clover. These goats will still require some rudimentary shelter, and must be of a very hardy type, such as the goats that are already running free in these areas. Some of them have been found to have a good cashmere undercoat, and this is removed in spring. Cashmere goats are also now coming into the country, for crossing with ferals, in order to produce a heavier crop of cashmere. Apart from this small amount of fibre, the only other income from ferals would be for the meat, and as I have mentioned, marketing this at present is not easy although things are improving.

To summarise—I feel that dairy goats are still likely to be the most profitable form of goatkeeping in the long term, providing that you can sell all your produce. Angora keeping is producing a large profit at present, but also needs considerable capital to set up. Feral goatkeeping requires the least capital, but also provides the lowest income at present.

CHAPTER TWELVE

GOATS ON THE SMALLHOLDING

So far I have written mainly about goatkeeping as a distinct enterprise, so in this chapter I will illustrate how well goats can tie in with other forms of farming or small enterprises like pedigree dog breeding.

The seasonality of goats' milk has always been a bugbear, and while it can be overcome to some extent, as we have seen, there is always a surplus of milk in the summer. Although there is very little profit to be made in producing goats' milk especially for animal use, it is a different matter when just using part of the summer flush or utilising by-products like whey and skim milk. In any case, with a free-range herd, the cost of production is at its lowest at that time of the year. If you can sell all your winter milk at a high price, it will not be a loss to have to use some of the summer production for stock rearing.

CALF REARING

One of the easiest ways of using up a spare gallon of milk a day is to rear a calf. If you rear calves anyway on your farm, you may wish to save your spare milk for small or sickly calves, or for starting all bought-in calves on for their first week or two, before changing them over gradually to powder. It may surprise you to hear that calves do well on goats' milk. This is because the fat and protein balance of cows' and goats' milk are about the same, but the latter is more quickly and easily digested, even for calves! When young calves are first bought from a market, they are suffering from a certain amount of stress, and as such their digestive systems are not in a state to cope with normal amounts of milk. Because of this many calf rearers give them a special formula, or a glucose drink for the first day, but we have found this unnecessary when goats' milk is available. They respond so well to it, that they are able to increase their consumption of milk much more quickly and yet safely. This means that they are often taking their full ration within a few days. If you do overfeed them, thus causing a simple milk scour, they recover very quickly if given a short rest from milk for one or two feeds.

Once the calf has had a chance to rest for a few hours after arrival on the farm, we usually give him a small feed of about two pints, and the same the following morning. If all goes well, this is gradually increased so that the calf is taking one gallon per day in two or three feeds. After that, the calf is reared as on any other normal system, and weaned onto calf concentrates fully at about six weeks or so, calf concentrates and hay having been offered from about a week old. If milk is still to spare, then you can continue to feed it as long as you wish, thus saving on some of the concentrates.

Many goatkeepers keep one calf to rear for their own beef. In this case, it is best to buy him in the spring, when he can be reared as cheaply as possible, using plenty of milk, grazing and only a minimum of concentrates. Providing that he does not attempt to suck, the calf can run out with the goats, as the two species carry different worms, each eating and thereby destroying the worm larvae of the other. If he does show interest in udders, then he could go out with youngstock, or be company for your stud male. Very cheap Jersey or Jersey/beef crosses are ideal for this purpose and make a good small carcass for the family if kept until the second autumn. The grazing habits of cattle are different too, and beef cattle in particular will find a great deal of grass in a field that the goats have finished with. Being impervious to rain, cattle can graze on longer into the winter, tidying up the grass so that it is short before the frosts come.

ORPHAN LAMBS

Sheep are not quite such an ideal grazing companion as cattle, only because they share a number of diseases and parasites. As long as you are aware of this and worm frequently, there should be no serious health problems unless your sheep happen to be carrying an enzootic abortion, or a disease like orf. Be careful of the latter when buying in orphan lambs, avoiding any with suspect spots on their faces. Keep the lambs entirely separate until you are sure that they are healthy, bearing in mind that they also suffer from the same sort of E. coli scour as young kids.

Many goatkeepers rear some orphan lambs on spare milk. If you have sheep anyway, it is likely that you will have some spare lambs to rear by hand and will find that they do very well on goats' milk. If you have to buy them in, it may be uneconomical because of the cost one is often expected to pay for the lamb. However, the price that you get for the finished animal will be better than that for a male kid, and this must be taken into consideration when deciding whether to put milk into lambs or kids. Lambs are fed just the same as the kids, on a teat and bottle or lamb-bar. It is wise to feed orphans four times daily, with just a little milk each time at first, or even more often if they are very weak. Goat colostrum is ideal for young lambs if they have failed to receive sufficient from their dams, and will often save a weak, cold lamb. Warming such lambs is all-important, and the time-honoured smallholder's method of bringing them into the kitchen seems as good as any other.

Goats' milk is not as rich as ewes' and the lamb will need slightly more in quantity to make up for this. A satisfactory amount seems to be 3pt (1.7L) a day, having only gradually increased to this amount. They only need milk feeding for about six to eight weeks and graze appreciable amounts of grass earlier than kids. One word of warning—be careful not to feed lambs, particularly male ones, on large quantities of concentrate other than that made especially for sheep. The mineral content of goat feeds is too high for lambs, and this can lead to stones in the bladder.

When the weather is suitable, the lambs can go out, and are soon able to remain out at night as well as day, if they have some simple shelter to get under. Once fully reared, they can either be killed for home use, sold in the market, or, in the case of ewe lambs, join the flock.

PIGS

Pigs of all ages do very well on goats' milk and by-products. Very small weaners, runt pigs and even orphans can be reared on goats' milk providing they have had some sow colostrum on the first day. The usual practice for smallholders is to buy a couple of weaners in spring. These will be ready for slaughter before the milk becomes in short supply again. It is difficult to be adamant about the amount of milk that can be fed to pigs as we have found that they seem to have an endless capacity! We give them barley meal or pig meal, soaked to a wet mash with milk, and to begin with, offer an amount that they will clear up quickly. This is gradually increased according to appetite. Pigs nearing slaughter weight can consume a gallon or more of milk, skim or whey, either on its own, or mixed to a sloppy meal with dry food. Adult sows, especially when in-pig or lactating, will also appreciate a trough of milk to drink. Non-intensive pigs, kept in a large pen, do very well on this diet of barley meal, which is usually the cheapest cereal, with milk or whey, but do take into account that the latter is not as nutritious as whole milk. Indoor pigs are supposed to be fed a mineral mixture, but we have found that providing they are fed ample vegetable scraps, and weeds with earth attached, it appears unnecessary. Outdoor pigs will find their own plants to root out and eat to provide all the minerals they need.

They are the most useful animals to keep in conjunction with a dairy herd, finishing up any kind of waste produce such as cheese which has gone wrong, stale yogurt and even very sour milk. Yogurt by the way is ideal for keeping bugs at bay when fed to newly arrived piglets. In addition to the dairy waste, pigs can consume spilled goat feed, wasted hay that has been pulled from the racks, and the same green food and roots that goats like, with the exception of the prickly and thorny items and evergreens like ivy.

KITTENS AND PUPPIES

It would seem that many young animals can be reared on goats' milk if orphaned, and we have sold milk for various babies from foals to kittens. The latter are not easy to bottle rear and you will probably only succeed with part of the litter if they are orphaned very young. Small feeding bottles for these tiny orphans can be purchased from pet shops. I must emphasise though, that goats' milk is not magical and will not successfully save all orphans.

Valuable pedigree kittens and puppies feeding from their mothers will benefit greatly from the addition of goats' milk to their diet, and you may be able to find regular customers among such breeders. Selling milk for animal consumption does not involve you in any regulations, and you can also ask the customer to provide his own containers, charging a lower price to take this into account.

A bitch rearing a large litter will be seen to rear them better while at the same time keeping herself in good condition if she has goats' milk, and the puppies can obviously have the milk to drink as soon as they are able. This will take the pressure off the mother. If you have a very large litter to rear, the pups can have additional feeds from a bottle from a few days old, to prevent one or two falling behind. These can be picked out for special attention.

GOATS AND GRASSLAND

I have dealt with the way in which goats benefit the other animals on the smallholding, but the land itself benefits as well. Some older farmers have the erroneous notion that goats are bad for a farm, but, apart from their destructive effect on hedges and trees, which must be curbed, this is simply not true. The facts show quite the reverse, as proved by the Hill Farming Research Unit in Scotland, who have shown what most goatkeepers know already, that goats improve grassland. They do not eat right down into the roots and crown of the grasses as sheep do, thereby allowing a faster regrowth after grazing. They relish a wide variety of weeds such as thistles and docks, which are particularly difficult to eradicate, and by restricting these undesirables, allow faster and better grass growth. Their dung encourages the proliferation of clover, of which they are not particularly fond. This heavy clover growth will then provide more nitrogen to grow still more grass. Because of this, when grazing with sheep or cattle, it has been shown that they actually make more grass available for these species, especially on rough land. Even on good-quality lowland grass, this benefit can be seen, but the effect is marked on the hills.

Goats prefer their grazing grass to be several inches long so it is no use putting them in a field after sheep or horses, and expecting them to survive on the few nettles left; they should always have first pick at a field, especially when milking.

Unless you have very extensive grazing and are understocked, fertilizer will be needed to ensure that the grass continues to grow well enough for both grazing and conservation of winter forage. The amount of fertilizer you use will vary according to circumstances and your policy for its use. We have had very good results from using one of the organically based fertilizers applied just once in the spring. This type of product continues to release nutrients slowly throughout the year, in the same way that natural manure does.

The manure from a goathouse is particularly rich, as you will discover when you begin to grow vegetables on it. It can improve a poor garden out of all recognition in a few seasons, whether the soil is light or heavy. It is also ideal for market gardening, being full of straw and far less strong smelling than pig or poultry manure. The usual way to manage the manure for the farm, is to pile it up as tidily as possible and have it spread on the fields in winter, ideally when the ground is hard with frost. Applied at this time, it will have all disappeared in time for spring grazing, and will continue to give out valuable nutrients to the grass for many months, usually enabling you to take a crop of hay or silage later on, as well as the early bite.

It would seem that at last the dairy goat has reached her proper and correct place in the scheme of British agriculture. She is no longer regarded as a pet owned only by old ladies or by hairy commune dwellers. Although her place as the basis for self-sufficiency is still as relevant as ever, she has reached a more general acceptability as a genuine farm animal. In these days of milk quotas and other restrictions on almost all conventional farm production, it may be the goat which provides hope of a profitable enterprise for many farmers' sons and daughters wishing to remain in agriculture. Providing that the individuality and character of this unique animal are never ignored and she is treated with dignity and respect, I can think of no better future for her.

USEFUL ADDDRESSES

The British Goat Society, 34–6 Fore Street, Bovey Tracy, Newton Abbot, Devon
The Goat Producers' Association, c/o AGRI, Shinfield, Reading, Berks
The British Angora Goat Society, Ash Farm, Iddesleigh, Winkleigh, Devon
The Goat Veterinary Society, c/o The Limes, Rettendon Common, Chelmsford, Essex

Suppliers of goatkeeping and dairying equipment
Lincolnshire Smallholders Suppliers Ltd., Thorpe Fendyke, Wainfleet, Lincolnshire
Harvester, Much Birch, Hereford, Herefordshire
Goat Nutrition, Tenterdon Road, Biddenden, Ashford, Kent
Fullwood and Bland, Ellesmere, Shropshire SY12 9DF

INDEX